JEWISH
CHOICES,
JEWISH
VOICES

SEX AND
INTIMACY

This book has been made possible by the
generosity of the

Everett Foundation

JEWISH
CHOICES,
JEWISH
VOICES

SEX AND INTIMACY

EDITED BY
ELLIOT N. DORFF
AND
DANYA RUTTENBERG

2010 • 5770
The Jewish Publication Society
Philadelphia

JPS is a nonprofit educational association and the oldest and foremost publisher of Judaica in English in North America. The mission of JPS is to enhance Jewish culture by promoting the dissemination of religious and secular works, in the United States and abroad, to all individuals and institutions interested in past and contemporary Jewish life.

The Jewish Publication Society
2100 Arch Street, 2nd floor
Philadelphia, PA 19103
www.jewishpub.org

Design and Composition by Progressive Information Technologies
Manufactured in the United States of America

09 10 11 12   10 9 8 7 6 5 4 3 2 1
ISBN: 978-0-8276-0860-3   (v.1. BODY)
ISBN: 978-0-8276-0861-0   (v.2. MONEY)
ISBN: 978-0-8276-0862-7   (v.3. POWER)
ISBN: 978-0-8276-0905-1   (v.4. SEX AND INTIMACY)

Library of Congress Cataloging-in-Publication Data:
Jewish choices, Jewish voices / edited by Elliot N. Dorff, Louis E. Newman. — 1st ed.
    v. cm.
    Includes bibliographical references and index.
    Contents: v. 1. Body
    ISBN 978-0-8276-0860-3 (BODY)
    1. Jewish ethics.   2. Jews—Identity.   3. Body, Human—Religious aspects—Judaism.   I. Dorff, Elliot N.   II. Newman, Louis E.

    BJ1285.2.J49 2008
    296.3'6—dc22   2007037402

CONTENTS

Acknowledgments

No book—let alone a series of books—comes about without the creative energy and support of many people. We wish to thank, first and foremost, Ellen Frankel, Editor Emerita of The Jewish Publication Society, for her vision in first conceiving of this series and for her willingness to entrust it to our editorship. The JPS National Council played a critical role early on as the scope and format of the series were in the development stage. Julia Oestreich was invaluable and indefatigable as the Project Manager of this volume, acting with care, thoroughness and thoughtfulness at every turn, helping us to keep track of what needed to be done, making wonderful suggestions about possible contributors, and providing us with astute and constructive comments about earlier drafts of every part of this volume, including our own writing. Along with the editors, Rabbis Uzi Weingarten and Steven Edelman-Blank collected, respectively, the classical and the contemporary Jewish sources for this volume. We are indebted to them for their fine work in locating these materials. We also wish to thank Monica Barr, Assistant Project Manager, who helped us immensely in contacting our contributors, making sure that they received and signed the proper contracts, and working with them to ensure that their contributions came in on time and that we had the latest versions of their essays in hand. We would additionally like to thank Julia Oestreich and Carol Hupping for their skillful copyediting work, including organizing and coordinating scores of details necessary to ready this volume for publication. Their diligence and attention to detail are evident on every page of this book. Finally, we especially want to thank our contributors, whose creativity and thoughtfulness make this anthology the stimulating and deeply Jewish book that it is.

E.N.D.
D.R.

Introduction

Come, my beloved,
Let us go into the open;
Let us lodge among the henna shrubs.
Let us go early to the vineyards;
Let us see if the vine has flowered,
If its blossoms have opened,
If the pomegranates are in bloom.
There I will give my love to you.
The mandrakes yield their fragrance,
At our doors are all choice fruits;
Both freshly picked and long-stored
Have I kept, my beloved, for you. (Songs 7:12–14)

JEWISH TRADITION understands the power of sex. Through laws and values, it tries to channel that power for good purposes for both the individual and society in general. It regards sex as God's gift to us, as a source of pleasure, as a way for a couple to bond and connect emotionally, and as the mechanism through which they might be blessed with children. The tradition also articulates the pain of sexual dysfunction, particularly in regard to infertility. Thus, the tradition veers mightily away from the extremes of regarding sex as the source of sin or of seeing it as simply a bodily function that has no more emotional or social import for those engaging in it than breathing or elimination.

Sex has been around since the beginning of humanity, and some of our issues with sex have just as old a pedigree. Many of the attitudes and behaviors of our ancestors remain influential today. For example:

- Sex has a potent effect on our lives for all three reasons mentioned above—for its physical pleasures, for its emotional meanings, and for its potential for procreation.
- At the same time, sex is not the whole of human life. This means that everyone must find a way to balance his/her sexuality and sex life with the many other parts of a whole life, including relationships, children, family, career, and involvement in social issues.

- Infertility has plagued couples who want to have children, just as it did the biblical Patriarchs and Matriarchs—Abraham and Sarah, Isaac and Rebekah, and Jacob and Leah and Rachel.

- Incest, adultery, and rape have been problems throughout human history, and the Babylonian Talmud even recognizes the possibility of marital rape and bans it (Eruvin 100b). One would surmise that other kinds of sexual abuse have been around for just as long, though they have been spoken about far less in Jewish sources.

- The "oldest profession," prostitution, is still thriving, but in many new forms that reflect shifting technology and transportation, and for many, a new sense of professionalism.

- Sexually transmitted diseases (STDs) have also undoubtedly been a part of human sexual activities from the beginning of the human species, but we know much more about them now and can cure some of them and control the spread of some others.

- Homosexual relations have also been part of human sexual history, since at least the ancient era. Yet, societies throughout history have had varying attitudes toward this phenomenon.

- Finally, while this is a matter that is hotly debated in our time, some maintain that the differences between men and women are not just a matter of their genitalia, but also of how they think and feel about sex, while others maintain that past and present social attitudes have had a much bigger impact than biology in this matter.

On the other hand, there are a number of circumstances affecting our sexual lives that differ from those of our ancestors:

- The status of women—economically, politically, socially, and religiously—has changed dramatically since the 1960s, and that has had a myriad of implications for how two adults negotiate a sexual relationship.

- Arranged marriages have given way to romantic relationships and active dating with, in many cases, "trial" relationships lasting several weeks, months, or longer.

- In times past, people commonly married in their late teens, but new educational, economic, and sociological realities have led many people to postpone marriage until their late 20s or early 30s—leading to a whole host of new sexual behaviors and norms.

- Some technological advances, such as effective birth control and safe and legal abortion, have affected the willingness of couples who do not want to marry or have children to have sexual relations nevertheless.

- STDs now include AIDS, which, though increasingly treatable, is still lethal.

- Recognition of same-sex and transgendered love and sexuality is increasing, with more and more states and nations giving legal status to same-sex marriage, domestic partnerships, or civil unions.

- Laws forbidding adultery, fornication, and masturbation have disappeared in the United States and in many other Western nations.

- The rate of divorce is considerably greater than it was in times past, especially among Jews. This raises issues about sex, love, and dating, not only for the couple, but also for any children they might have produced or adopted.

More broadly, feminist and queer approaches to sexuality and new understandings of masculinity have opened up new avenues of thinking and new ways to approach sexuality. We are increasingly asking ourselves questions such as: Why do we believe what we believe about sexuality? To what extent is our perception of sexuality built into our nature, and to what extent is it a socially constructed set of expectations? What are other possible lenses through which we might regard our sexual lives and possibilities? Does sexual identity matter? Can it be fluid? Should the norms for sexual activity be the same for gays and lesbians as they are for straight people? Is monogamy a virtue in either dating or marriage? To what extent should procreation be a goal of sex?

Also, women are now getting the same level of education as men, and are beginning to access the same level of jobs that only men have historically held. How does this change our understanding of what it means to be a man or a woman?

Think of changing standards of censorship for books, movies, and TV programs over the last 60 years, and the influence of the Internet over the last 15 years. To what extent is sexual activity now already—and to what extent should it be—acceptable in the public domain, and to what extent should it be restricted to private quarters?

As modern Jews, our thinking is influenced by both Western culture and Jewish heritage. Sometimes they tell us the same things about how to live our lives, and sometimes they have radically different messages for us. Thus, even someone who wants to lead a deeply traditional life has to apply the Jewish tradition to modern circumstances that are significantly different from those of times past, and so one inevitably has to make judgments about how to do that. It is not as easy as simply citing the chapter and verse of a biblical text or a code of Jewish law. And for those of us who live more firmly in the modern world, the questions are even more complex. The less that one uses Jewish heritage as a source of sexual values, the more that one has to look elsewhere for such moral guidance in choosing his/her own particular values and behaviors.

And yet, Judaism can give us important insights if we know how to access its lessons and values. This book is an attempt to help foster that process.

Neither the cases in this volume nor the sources we cite are meant to be exhaustive, for there are problems in the area of human sexuality that we did not have space to treat—some of which are mentioned in passing above—and there are sources that we did not have space to include. Nonetheless, we hope that the cases, sources and responses that we did include will form a helpful foundation for readers to negotiate the issues in human sexuality that we do address directly, as well as those we do not, using the Jewish tradition as at least one source of values. In the end, after all, we are sexual beings, and for all the problems that sex entails, it also can be the source of physical and emotional fulfillment—indeed, the gift from God that the Jewish tradition portrays it as being.

CASE 1

❧

DATING ETHICS

Case Study

ON A university campus, Pat has been dating Sam for two months, while Alex has gone out with Jamie five times in the last two weeks. Neither Pat and Sam, nor Alex and Jamie have had conversations establishing a monogamous, exclusive relationship, but in both cases, some assumptions have been made about their status as couples. One day, Alex and Pat meet, and notice an immediate chemistry; Pat asks Alex out, and Alex accepts. Does Pat have an obligation to say something to Sam? Does Alex have an obligation to Jamie? Under what circumstances is it fair to presume exclusivity? When, if at all, does one have a duty to inform someone with whom she or he is romantically involved about the possibility of dating someone else? Why? Does it matter whether Pat and Alex have had sex with Sam and Jamie, respectively? Does the obligation to inform Sam and/or Jamie change if Alex and Pat:

a) had sex as a one-night stand?

b) went on a date with the intention to see if there was relationship potential but did not have sex?

c) went on a date to see if there was relationship potential and had sex?

Does any of this change if Alex and Pat's original relationships were heterosexual and this new coupling was a same-sex relationship? What if Alex and Pat's original relationships were same-sex and this new coupling is heterosexual?

If Pat and Sam have been dating for two years, with talk of possible marriage, and Pat decides that she or he wants to explore other relationships before committing to Sam, how does that affect Pat's obligations to Sam? Sam's obligations to Pat? What if Pat and Sam are already married at the time that Pat and Alex meet? At the other end of the spectrum, what if Alex and Jamie had just had a one-night stand and are leaving open the possibility that there might be more—do they have any obligations to each other? If so, what are they?

If Alex and Jamie have an established relationship but have agreed not to be monogamous, what are their duties to each other?

Traditional Sources

Compiled by Uzi Weingarten and the Editors

On the Duty to Treat Others with Love and Respect

1. Babylonian Talmud, *Shabbat* 31a

Hillel said: What you detest, do not do to your fellow. This is the entire Torah, all of it. The rest is commentary. Go study!

2. *Sifra* 7:2 on Leviticus 19:18 (and quoted by Rashi there)

"Love your neighbor as yourself": Rabbi Akiva says: This is a great principle of the Torah.

3. Babylonian Talmud, *Makkot* 24a

Moses received 613 commandments at Sinai ... Micah (6:8) came and stood them on three: "Do justice, love kindness, and walk with your God humbly."

On Sex Outside of Marriage

4. Mishnah, *Ketubbot* 1:5

One who eats at his [future] father-in-law's house [during the year between betrothal and marriage] in [the land of] Yehudah without witnesses cannot [after the wedding night] make a claim against his fiancee's virginity.

5. Babylonian Talmud, *Yevamot* 51b

Rabbi Yehudah said: A *zonah* [a prostitute, licentious woman] is one who is infertile. But the Sages said: No one is considered a *zonah* save a convert, or a liberated slave, or one who has had forbidden sexual relations [i.e., engaged in a forbidden sexual partnering, such as incest or adultery].

Rabbi Elazar said: If a single man comes to a single woman [for sexual relations] without the intention of marriage, he makes her into a *zonah*.

Rabbi Amram said: The law is not according to Rabi Elazar.

6. Babylonian Talmud, *Gittin* 81b

The House of Shammai say that a man [is willing to] make his acts of sexual intercourse the intercourse of licentiousness, while the House of Hillel say that a man does not [want to] make his acts of intercourse the intercourse of licentiousness.

4

Note: Elsewhere in the Talmud, in *Yevamot* 107a and *Ketubbot* 73a, only the House of Hillel's position is quoted, with no indication that there is any dispute in the matter.

7. Maimonides (Rambam), *Mishneh Torah*, Laws of Divorce 10:19

A few of the Geonim [heads of the Babylonian rabbinic academies between 650 and 1050 C.E.] taught that any woman who sleeps with a man before witnesses [that the two entered a room together alone] needs a writ of divorce because we presume that a man does not want to make his acts of sexual intercourse acts of licentiousness.... But all of these rulings are, in my opinion, very far from the paths of proper instruction, and one should not depend on them. For the Sages announced this presumption only with regard to his wife whom he divorced, or if he betrothed a woman on condition and slept with her without that condition being met, for then [in either of those two cases] she is his wife, and regarding his wife we have the presumption that he would not want his acts of sexual intercourse to be acts of licentiousness unless he specifies that he intends to engage in an act of licentiousness with her or that he is sleeping with her on condition; but with regard to other women, we assume that he had sexual intercourse with any licentious woman for the sake of licentiousness unless he specifies that his act of sexual intercourse is for the purpose of betrothing her.

8. Rabbi Abraham ben David (Ravad), comment on Maimonides' *Mishneh Torah*, Laws of Divorce 10:19

We view the sons and daughters of Israel according to what we presume about them, and they are under the presumption that they act in fitting ways (*b'hezkat kashrut hen*), so they would not act licentiously before witnesses to engage in licentiousness.

9. Rabbi Moses Isserles, comment on *Shulchan Arukh, Even Ha-Ezer* 33:1

There are those who say that if a single man had sexual intercourse with a single woman before witnesses, we wonder whether he intended to do this for the sake of betrothing her, for we presume that a man does not want to make his acts of sexual intercourse acts of licentiousness. But if he was already presumed to engage in licentiousness or if he had another wife, we do not wonder about this.

10. Babylonian Talmud, *Yevamot* 37b

Rab, whenever he happened to visit [the town of] Dardeshir, used to announce, "Who would be mine for the day?" So also R. Nahman, whenever he happened to visit Shekunzib, used to announce, "Who would be mine for the day?"

On Honesty in Sexual Relations

11. Maimonides (Rambam), *Mishneh Torah*, Laws of Ethics 2:6

One may not conduct himself with smooth, seductive words, and one may not say one thing and think something else, but rather "his inner [should be] like his outer," and what is in his thoughts should be what is on his lips. And one may not steal another's thinking ... for example, he may not offer his friend a gift if he knows that his friend does not accept gifts [thus gaining goodwill without having truly offered anything] ... Rather, [one should utter only] true speech and [have] an honest spirit and a heart pure of all wrongdoing.

12. Mishnah, *Kiddushin* 2:3 (in the Babylonian Talmud, *Kiddushin* 49b)

[A man who betroths a woman] "with the stipulation that I am a Cohen" and it turns out he is a Levite ... "that I live close to the public bathhouse" and it turns out he lives far away, "with the stipulation that I do not have children" and it turns out that he does ... even if she said I had in mind to become betrothed [regardless], she is not betrothed. And so too if she misled him.

13. Exodus 20:14; Deuteronomy 5:18

You shall not covet your neighbor's wife.

14. Babylonian Talmud, *Berakhot* 19b

[So] great [a concern] is human dignity that it overrides a Torah prohibition.

Contemporary Sources

Compiled by Steven Edelman-Blank

1. Michael Strassfeld, *A Book of Life: Embracing Judaism as a Spiritual Practice* (New York: Schocken Books, 2002), 369

Of course, honesty must be the common language of sexual partners. Whether being misleading in order to get someone into bed or being untruthful about your commitment, these are forms of lying. Lies can also be what is hidden, such as secretly being involved with someone else. You need not be in a marriage for an affair to be a betrayal of an understanding of commitment and trust between two people.

Finally, even when not secretive, promiscuity or one-night stands challenge anyone's ability to treat sexuality as a form of holiness. Is it possible for sex to be just sex, a physical act of release and pleasure? Possibly, but most of the time there is an emotional element involved, at least for one of the partners. It is rarely just the equivalent of eating a good meal, much as we might try to pretend otherwise. Once there is more at stake, all the ethical principles come into play. Ultimately we need to acknowledge sexuality as a powerful force that also provides the opportunity for two people to touch the deepest parts of each other's being.

2. Robert Gordis. *Love and Sex: A Modern Jewish Perspective.* (New York: Women's League for Conservative Judaism, 1978), 105

The sex-love relationship is not complete unless it is accompanied by a feeling of permanence. It is not an act of deception or even honest hyperbole that impels lovers to swear that their love will endure forever. What is deep and all-inclusive will not be satisfied without the conviction that it will endure.

3. Maurice Lamm, *The Jewish Way in Love and Marriage* (Middle Village, New York: Jonathan David Publishers, Inc., 1991), 25

Today there is no talk of standards, God's or society's. It seems sex is all right in every form—so long as it is not repressed, Freud forbid. We are faced with this question: What shall sex be used for now that it is no longer tied to that sacred, cosmically significant function of perpetuating the family, the faith, and the human race? Society's answer seems to be very simple: fun—and fun has no rules.

4. Elizabeth Heubeck, "The Dating Game: When's the Right Time for Sex?" Available at http://www.webmd.com/sex/features/sex-dating-rules?page=2

Once you've decided what you want out of a date, say experts, you should make it part of your regular dating rules to tell your partner.

7

"If you just want a one-night stand, you owe it to your partner to tell them 'it's just sex I'm after,'" McClary tells WebMD. While a dating partner may not welcome this news, it at least can minimize later disappointments.

5. **Ruth K. Westheimer and Jonathan Mark.** *Heavenly Sex: Sexuality in the Jewish Tradition* **(New York: New York University Press, 1995), 6**

Good sex is inseparable from good communication, which is sensitive and kind communication. Today we teach women to be assertive. But if a woman says to her partner, "Either you get it up or I'm leaving," he is not going to have an erection, and she will be left as disappointed as Madam Potiphar.

Responses

Seeing Each Other and Seeing Ourselves: Jewish Ethical Dating in the Modern Age

Esther D. Kustanowitz

Sex—Then and Now

RUMOR HAS it that dating used to be easy. If you—a man—liked a woman, you bonked her on the head and dragged her back to your cave. This was known as "going steady." When you didn't want her anymore, you kicked her out of her cave and let her fend off the T. rexes or other wild beasts. This was known as "seeing other people."

Then, a little later, there was the biblical model: send your servant to track down your cousins at the local well. How will you know they are your intended? They will offer you a drink, and then offer to water your camels (a clear euphemism for something), or, when you roll the rock off the well, the waters will rise up to meet you. Occasionally, you will have to work for your future father-in-law to earn the betrothal, but honest work is a good thing, and how long could that take, anyway?

Defining commitment was simpler, if somewhat less freely chosen by the woman: man finds woman in his favor, and as it says in Deuteronomy 24:1, he "takes a wife and possesses her." Sexual union was generally considered the same thing as matrimonial union. Certainly, it didn't have to mean that the man was then limited to only one woman, as polygamy was *de rigeur*, especially for men who wanted many children, or more variety. And often, such an additional spouse (or spouses) of valor could be found within the immediate family. Rachel and Leah's lives, for instance, were something like HBO's polygamy series *Big Love*, but with their blood sisters as their "sister-wives."

Not surprisingly, many people today don't identify with the traditional "meet at the well, marry, have children and trek through the desert of life together" model. Western society largely frowns on polygamy, and the ethics involved in declaring relationships publicly and in varying degrees of exclusivity are proportionally more complicated.

Today we have to deal with things like attraction, the dating preferences of both genders instead of mainly the man's, compatibility of religious level, height, making sure you are NOT related, and occasionally other issues, like JDate photographs that may or may not reflect our actual appearance, spammed emails, and missed text messages. Plus, if we are having sex before marriage, we have to inquire uncomfortably about our partner's sexual history and insist on safe sex (ideally—although not everyone does).

And then there is the relatively recent redefinition of marriage as only between one man and one woman, a characterization that has come under scrutiny, most notably and controversially in the outrage over California's Proposition 8. People who urged a "no" vote on 8 were in favor of permitting same-sex partners to be legally married. The "yes on 8" segment, funded heavily by the Mormon church, urged California voters to preserve what they viewed as the traditional definition of marriage: one man, one woman. (It's worth noting that none of our biblical forefathers would have embraced that definition either, as until the *takkanah* of Rabbeinu Gershom around 1000 C.E., polygamy was completely legal for Jews, and became legal again when that law expired in 2000.) Unfortunately, our wells just aren't the singles scene they used to be.

Add to the mix the contemporary romantic expectations set by TV, film and other media of hearing violins and being swept away by a "meet-cute" or love at first sight, and our expectations go haywire. Then add online dating, with its perception of infinite choice and romance made-to-order, which succeeds for some while making so many others even more resentful. Most Jews today who do not live in self-selecting enclaves live in this more assimilated social context, surrounded by Jews of varying levels of religious observance, as well as non-Jews, and affected by the outside world. Among the messages that filter in are the media's definitions of beauty and attraction, influences about when (if at all) to marry, how many children (if any) to have, and modern criticisms of why a person might or might not be the perfect mate. And people who hail from traditional religious backgrounds may not have the sexual education background necessary for making smart decisions about what to do with whom, both before and during a marriage.

While Orthodox day school education often focuses on Jewish values, sexuality in general is avoided as a subject matter. Some of the sexually complicated biblical narratives are reframed or skipped, and because practical sex education is minimal, if existent at all, many young observant Jews grow up without the comprehension of their own (and others') equipment and its responses to various environmental stimuli. Even educators who provide basic sex-ed seldom place unmarried sexual activity within a Jewish ethical perspective, the implication being that sex has no role outside of marriage and should not—and by omission from the curriculum, will not—occur.

Creating a Jewish Sex Ethic

Whether a relationship actually works to the satisfaction of both parties depends on creating a set of rules that helps to define what the relationship is or is not. But beyond defining the parameters of such an arrangement, honest communication and mutual consideration are elements that can transform any relationship from something casual, or even potentially sordid, into something more ethical.

Sometimes people view themselves as romantically committed to a person without feeling the need to define that commitment as exclusive. But in a culture where we're constantly defining ourselves in a context of having multiple identities, there is also a whole litany of ways to define sexual relationships. Many people eschew approved, traditional labels politically, religiously and socially, and do the same with romantic liaisons unless both parties are looking for the same level of commitment. But singles can't even agree on what the language of commitment is. Is "seeing each other" or "dating" the more serious expression of commitment?

The parameters of commitment are different, but often include agreement on exclusivity. While there is certainly an emotional component to exclusivity, when modern non-Orthodox couples (and frankly, even some Orthodox couples) talk about exclusivity, they mean sexclusivity. For some people, sexual congress is a major deal, a non-verbal expression of commitment whether or not exclusivity has been discussed. But for others, it's just another Thursday night. (Talk about it before you do it? Call the next day? Whatever for? It was only sex...)

Many ethical principles found in biblical and talmudic texts should apply in all sorts of modern contexts, including dating. Whether you view the text as Divine or divinely inspired, or just want to be more considerate of others, imagining everyone as having been created *b'tzelem Elohim*—in the image of God, and therefore possessing a bit of the divine that renders us all equally worthy—can inspire greater respect toward the people with whom we share the planet. This equality keeps us grounded to our common bond as humans, even as it reminds us to behave in a more divine way.

The people in our case may not lack a commitment to commitment, but they may be lacking the commitment to conversation. While rocking

11

a perfectly good boat is an understandable fear, if the person you are looking at is a potential partner for life, working out how to have a discussion about something difficult is a vital skill. Are you allowed to go see your ex who is going through a bad time and keep that from your partner? Does it hurt him or her more to know about it, or to not know about it? Is phone sex or cybersex cheating? Does it matter if you know who you are having sexual relations with or if it's all anonymous? If civilizations form around a shared set of values and behavioral expectations, how do you identify the ethical geography of your relationship? How can you expect to know the answers to any of these questions unless they are specifically discussed?

At bare minimum, the Torah seems to tell us, there is the injunction not to stand idly by the blood of your neighbor (Lev. 19:16). While this can certainly be read as a commandment against endangering your partner, a figurative reading also provides some contemporary resonance. According to texts, blood doesn't just mean literal blood spilling forth from a wounded body, but also the blood that rushes to our faces when we become embarrassed. The word *adom*, meaning "red" in Hebrew, contains the word *dam*, which means "blood." When we are literally or emotionally wounded, we redden. Hence our lesson is to not be the inflictors of wounds that cause such reddening, either through literal or emotional methods. People who have not defined the borders of their relationships should not be surprised when their significant others end up defining them differently. They may unintentionally end up wounding each other.

Hillel told us to do unto others as you would have them do unto you (Babylonian Talmud, Shab. 31a). Would you like to be treated the way you are treating others when it comes to dating and relationships? If your answer is no, a self-assessment may be in order. Then there is the much-loved phrase, *"kol yisrael arevim zeh lazeh,"* or "all the people of Israel are responsible for each other" (Babylonian Talmud, Shevu. 39a). This kind of nationalistic appeal takes humanity from the general to the particular, in case that kind of appeal strikes a greater resonance with the modern Jewish dater.

"You shall not … place a stumbling block before the blind," the Torah tells us (Lev. 19:14). There is always a temptation to be literal with biblical text, but taking a more figurative approach also indicts those who deceive others: convince your fellow that things are other than what they seem to be and you have caused both their blindness and their fall. A policy of honest communication between partners about the nature and depth of their relationship keeps the playing field level. Both partners go from blind to sighted, and no unforeseen obstacles lie in their paths.

I have always believed that sexual ethics should be the same for all human beings, whether they are involved in casual sex, a friends with benefits situation, or committed partnerships of any sort with anyone of any gender, and that for all of these groups, communication about the nature of the relationship should take place in advance of sexual union. But anecdotally, evidence seems to point to the fact that people feel awkward talking about their relationships, especially in a moment when passions are running high and logical honesty is ... not so much. Most people agree that it's not the act of consummation that creates a committed relationship. If there has been no conversation to define a dyad, it can not be considered exclusive.

Communication and Commitment

If a couple of any gender combination is involved in an ongoing, committed relationship, however defined, and one partner wants to see someone else, I think there is a moral obligation to have a conversation. Beyond the health concerns of introducing another person's sexual history into the mix, by keeping secrets from a significant other you make that new liaison more significant, because you know it's wrong—you know you are stepping out on someone who is committed to you. And if the new person you are drawn to is of a different gender than your original partner, that also may have implications for the futures of both relationships.

I believe that commitment is commitment. Even more so, I view matrimony as a commitment that is inviolable. But recently I was reminded that not everyone has the same barometer for what is considered commitment. I had dinner with a potential business associate, a married man with children. Suddenly, over the course of dinner, our business seemed to veer into funny business. First came a few compliments, most of them professionally related. Then he asked to hold my hand. I told him no, and that he had made me uncomfortable, but that didn't stop him. He told me it was simple affection and I was over-interpreting it, but I think my yeshiva day school background spoke up at that moment. Years of learning about drawing fences around areas of temptation, creating moats and walls that kept sin in the barely visible distance, suddenly made sense. But in that more compromising position, in that moment of a potential breach in a protective fence, I was uncomfortable.

Since that hot summer night, I have wondered what I'd done to convey that there was possibility there, or whether I overreacted at a display of affection that perhaps, as he kept claiming, wasn't what I perceived it to be. I pondered how similar the actions of hand-shaking and hand-holding were, and tried to revisit the events from alternate perspectives. I put myself in his shoes, giving him the benefit of the doubt that he was expressing an intended affection-minus-sexual-desire only to be rejected. I stepped into his wife's loving and trusting shoes, and wondered how I would feel if my husband, the father of my children, was in a foreign city and held the hand of his younger, female, single potential business partner over dinner and wine.

Maybe this kind of thing happened all the time for him and his wife. If so, perhaps it wasn't a violation of their commitment, and therefore, strictly speaking, within their understanding of morality. Or maybe they had an open relationship that permitted liaisons on foreign soil. I put on my yeshiva girl glasses and thought to myself, this is why people are *shomer negiah*, and don't touch members of the opposite sex until they are married to one; because "good touch" can turn to "uncomfortable touch" while a wineglass empties. But regardless of any subjective moral codes or extenuating circumstances between him and his wife, for me this action on his part represented a crack in their commitment. And that made me uncomfortable.

I believe in honest communication, and have high standards once commitment is proclaimed. And because I know not everyone mirrors my constant commitment to commitment and communication, I try to keep my expectations (and sexpectations) in check, while keeping my standards high. It's a hard line to walk, and this line is probably part of what has kept me single. This is something that I, and probably other single Jews, struggle with, and is sometimes categorized among the frustrated as "unrealistic expectations."

Where are our models for contemporary Jewish dating? Maybe we need a liturgy that gives us the words to praise the divine elements of dating, or a *Shulchan Arukh* (code of Jewish law) that instructs us how to behave. Every Passover we read about being commanded to "see ourselves as if we came out of Egypt," about identifying personally with an ancient story and people. By seeing ourselves there, we can begin to understand what their lives were like and the choices they made.

I believe that by keeping in our hearts the injunction—whether divine, rabbinic, or personal—to treat others as we would like to be treated, and by clearly communicating our intentions, we elevate our dating behavior to a higher ethical level. We—or at least I—can only hope that at the end of the dating process, this approach will yield a more concerned, communicative, and ethical partner to stand at our side as we conquer the world. To put it another way, by elevating the way we see each other while we're seeing each other, we will more fully be able to see ourselves.

Doing What Is Right and Good
Uzi Weingarten

W HAT MAKES responding to the questions in this case study complicated is that there is so much we do not know. Who are Alex and Sam and Jamie and Pat? What are their backgrounds, and what assumptions do they, and their cultural environments, make about romantic relationships?

Changed Realities and the Relevance of Tradition

The sources in the Tradition can be of some help in answering these questions. However, our reality regarding these matters is so drastically different from that of the Sages that we need to apply the ancient teachings with great discernment. In the true process of *halakhah*, one doesn't just quote sources; one also applies them to current realities. This can be challenging, and when it comes to sexuality even more so, because the changes in this area, even in our own lifetimes, have been so dramatic.

One major example is that, in antiquity, a father arranged for his children's marriage: "I gave this man my daughter to wife" (Deut. 22:16). This was ideally done "close to their time," that is, shortly after the children entered puberty. By arranging for the children's marriage at that age, the father provided a framework for ethical, sacred expression of the natural sexual urges that arise at that time: "The Sages commanded that one marry off his sons and daughters close to their time, lest they come to sexual immorality or impure thoughts" (Maimonides [Rambam], *Mishneh Torah*, Laws of Forbidden Intercourse 21:25, based on the Babylonian Talmud, Yev. 62b, Sanh. 76b).

A more commonly known teaching is: "At 18, to the wedding canopy" (Mishnah, Avot 5:21). There were times that, due to less abundant nutrition, women arrived at puberty later, sometimes even as late as 17. This may explain the suggested age for marriage. Regardless, marrying children off at 18, as is still common in the Hasidic world, usually prevents many, though not all, of the questions this essay addresses from ever arising.

Today, however, young people wishing to marry at 18 or 20 would be hard-pressed to support a family. Gone are many of the manufacturing jobs and family businesses that once allowed high-school graduates to be financially self-sufficient. Increasingly, a college degree and even a graduate degree are prerequisites for a comfortable standard of living. Often, even those are not enough, and one needs a certain number of years at a given position to start earning a salary that could support a family with children.

The Tradition itself reminds us of the folly of entering into marriage before finances are in place: "The way of the wise is to first find work that supports him, then buy a house, then get married ... But the fools first get married, then look for housing, and lastly look for work" (Maimonides [Rambam], *Mishneh Torah*, Laws of Ethics 5:11). We thus have an almost unprecedented number of young adults financially unable to marry for a decade or more after puberty, a time of peak sexual desire for men, and often for women. How tragic that our wealthy society has brought about this situation, in which economics leave young adults with no choice but to delay marriage.

Another changed reality has to do with the context in which physical intimacy takes place. There has been a huge shift in what society considers moral. This is partially a result of the diminished impact of religious teachings, and partially a result of the advances in and accessibility of contraception. With the easy availability of birth control, which set the sexual revolution into motion, young adults are largely able to avoid the negative consequences that until recently accompanied, and often deterred, sex outside of marriage (i.e., social stigma and unwanted pregnancies).

So with the reality so different from that of the Sages, what can the Tradition still offer us as guidance?

First, there are broad statements of Jewish values that guide us in the dynamics of all interpersonal relationships, including romance and sexuality:

> What you detest, do not do to your fellow. This is the entire Torah, all of it. The rest is commentary. Go study! (Babylonian Talmud, Shab. 31a)

> "Love your neighbor as yourself": Rabbi Akiva says: This is a great principle of the Torah. (Sifra, quoted by Rashi about Lev. 19:18)

> Moses received 613 commandments at Sinai ... Micah (6:8) came and brought them down to three: "Do justice, love kindness, and walk humbly with your God." (Babylonian Talmud, Mak. 24a)

These three teachings have particular significance since they are each presented as summarizing the entire Torah. They can thus offer us guidance when more specific teachings are absent.

Applying them to the questions raised in the case study, when two people date, they should consider how to conduct themselves in romantic and sexual matters. They each might ask: What constitutes behavior "that I detest" and that I thus am not to do to another? What is included and precluded by the call to "do justice and love kindness" or by the mitzvah to act lovingly toward another?

Honesty

The Tradition offers some answers, beginning with the value of honesty. The Torah recognizes situations when "white lies" are permitted, most notably to promote harmony. But in situations where the other party has a right to know, it ordinarily forbids outright deception. I recognize a "right to know" as existing when one person is giving something or entering into a commitment. In a romantic relationship, each person is indeed giving something, emotional and physical intimacy, and is forgoing the opportunity to pursue other options. Thus, each partner has a right to know critical information. So, if one asks directly if the other considers their connection a committed relationship, or if the other had an affair, or is using contraceptives, or is infected with an STD, or has a family history of a given illness, it is unacceptable to lie.

Deception is not only carried out with words, however. One person may not deliberately act with the intention of giving an erroneous impression—what we would call "leading a person on"—even if nothing is said. The Tradition refers to this as *genevat da'at*, literally, stealing another's thinking. Here is a succinct summary of this principle:

> One may not conduct oneself with smooth, seductive words, and may not say one thing and think something else, but rather "his inside [should be] like his outside," so that what is in his thoughts is what is on his lips. And one may not steal another's thinking ... For example, one may not offer one's friend a gift if one knows that the friend does not accept gifts [thus gaining goodwill without having truly offered anything] ... Rather, [one should be of] true speech, an honest spirit, and a heart pure of all wrongdoing." (Maimonides [Rambam], *Mishneh Torah,* Laws of Ethics 2:6)

Thus, one who acts in a way that, by commonly accepted standards, implies romantic commitment has an obligation to clarify the truth to the other. One cannot simply claim, "I never said we were going steady." Actions speak louder than words, especially in matters of the heart. If in such a situation one had an affair on the side, it would, at the very least, involve deception, but its impact would mean much more than that of a simple betrayal.

Of course, the key is those "commonly accepted standards." They are what make it legitimate for one person to assume commitment. Otherwise, the betrayed party may have been engaging in wishful thinking and cannot then complain about being deceived. In the words of the Tradition: "He is misleading himself" (Babylonian Talmud, Ḥul. 94b).

The subject of romantic and sexual relationships is so tricky precisely because there are no hard and fast rules, and there are huge gray areas that could lead to heartbreak for one or both people. Applying the principles of deception and self-deception that we have just discussed, is it legitimate to assume that a given period of time or a given number of dates establishes a *de facto* "committed relationship"? Or that in this age of STDs everybody uses contraceptives? Or takes tests to check for STDs? Or are these cases of what the Tradition means when it says, "he misled himself," that is, where one person made an unwarranted assumption?

Communication and Disclosure
Because these cues are ambiguous, the couple has an obligation to discuss the nature of the relationship early on. It is difficult to pinpoint the moment at which such a discussion needs to take place. Ideally, it should precede sexual activity (or a second sexual encounter if the first happened in the heat of the moment). Sexual involvement dramatically changes the dynamics of the connection, and both people need to enter that phase with a clear sense of where they stand.

There are additional reasons for this obligation. A woman who engages in sexual activity releases oxytocin, the "bonding hormone." It is the same hormone women secrete when nursing a baby. Men do not have a similar chemical response to sex. Thus, a sexual encounter often leaves a woman feeling bonded to a man. If he does not feel similarly about her, she experiences the pain of oxytocin withdrawal, and this can last up to two years. So for the woman, caution before engaging in sexual activity is a matter of her emotional well-being. For the man, knowing that this is how women respond is yet one more reason why discussing the nature of the relationship, in advance of sex, is an obligation.

This "right to know" is not limited to romantic and sexual matters, as this teaching tells us:

> [One who betroths a woman] "with the stipulation that I am a Cohen," and it turns out he is a Levite ... "that I live close to the public bathhouse," and it turns out he is far, "with the stipulation that I do not have children," and it turns out he does ... even if she said I had in mind to become betrothed [regardless], she is not betrothed. And so too if she misled him." (Mishnah, Kid. 2:3; Babylonian Talmud, Kid. 49b)

The issues here are not related to romantic commitment or to sexuality, but rather to lifestyle and to whom a prospective spouse is related. Nevertheless, betrothal is a contract and is thus nullified by deception. As I mentioned earlier, a partner is giving something (physical and emotional intimacy) and forgoing something (the right to have those with others), and thus has the right to know the truth.

It is interesting that this understanding is inherent in the English word "betrothal," as well. "Troth" is the Old English form of the word "truth," and to "be-troth" a woman is to "take her into one's truth." So the question of whether or not a partner has a "right to know" applies to a sexual encounter, to a long-term monogamous relationship, and to a marriage.

Adultery and Other Betrayals

Of course, the prohibition against adultery is one of the Ten Commandments: "You shall not covet your neighbor's wife" (Exod. 20:13,14; Deut. 5:17,18). Then there are things that technically may not be adultery but are surely a betrayal of the "covenant" of marriage: a woman has phone sex or Internet sex with another man, for example, or a man is physical with another woman but without intercourse. From a strictly legal standpoint, these do not constitute adultery in Jewish law because there was no penetration involved.

However, there is a verse of great significance, proclaimed by the last of the Hebrew prophets: "Because the LORD is a witness between you and the wife of your youth with whom you have broken faith, though she is your partner and your covenanted spouse" (Mal. 2:14). Betrayal is about more than what is included in the narrow definition of adultery. When two people enter into the covenant of marriage and pledge themselves to each other, they do not have in mind the narrow definition of adultery (i.e., penetration) as the only thing that will undermine their relationship. They are pledging themselves to a loving relationship that is both physically and emotionally monogamous.

A long-term relationship between two unmarried people cannot technically involve adultery, for that legal category applies only to married couples. But such relationships can most definitely involve betrayal: the betrayal of the commitment partners have made to each other through their words and their actions. And such betrayal is roundly condemned by the Jewish tradition. Judaism demands that we make our commitments clear and then honor them.

Dignity

No discussion on sexual relationships would be complete without mentioning the great importance that the Jewish tradition places on human dignity (Hebrew, *kavod ha-beriyot*): "Human dignity is [so] great that it overrides a Torah prohibition" (Babylonian Talmud, Ber. 19b, *et al.*). By way of comparison, only saving a human life ordinarily trumps Torah prohibitions. To be sure, the later talmudic sages (often referred to as the "Stam") limited the scope of this teaching when they ruled that human dignity overrides only rabbinic, not Torah, prohibitions. Even so, we still see the great weight attached to this value.

It is clear that actions that shame, belittle, or demean someone have no place in a healthy sexual relationship. As I mentioned earlier, men and women have different chemical responses to sexual intimacy. It is often said that women give sex for love, and men give love for sex. While in today's society this is far from universally true, there are still many women who engage in sexual activity with an implicit understanding that they will receive love and affection in return. When that does not happen, a woman might feel "cheap" or "used," left with the sinking feeling that she gave of her emotions and received nothing in return. Is it morally acceptable to have pleasure at the expense of another person's shame?

Doing What Is Right and Good

There is one more general teaching that bears mentioning here. The medieval commentator Nahmanides (Ramban, 13th-century Spain) offers

21

a profound elaboration on the verse: "Do what is right and good in the sight of the LORD" (Deut. 6:18). He says that no amount of legislation can cover every single situation because there will always be one more variable or nuance to be considered. So the Torah offers a long list of specific and general instructions, and then tells us to "do what is right and good in the eyes of the LORD." That is, we are to build on both the general principles and specific laws that we see in the Tradition, and then extrapolate from them the guidance we need to do the right thing.

I opened by saying that there is so much we do not know about Alex, Sam, Jamie, and Pat, and the cultural environment in which they operate. For that reason, I have offered general guidelines and specific teachings from the Tradition that help to address the issues their situation raises. It is my call to the readers of this essay to consider these teachings and to guide themselves in a way that is "right and good." Any pleasure, and certainly that which is gained by deceit, is momentary. But the satisfaction one gains from acting honorably, the self-esteem that comes from knowing that we live in accordance with our values, endures.

Sex, Truth, and Ethical Communication

S. Bear Bergman

U NFORTUNATELY, most of us Americans are not that comfortable talking about sex and sexual ethics. Of course, there are extremists, with one chorus shouting about sex, "Don't! Not Until Marriage!" and a smaller but no less excitable group hollering, "Go For It! Always!" Like most extremists, their positions are often oversimplified, but this makes them very easy to articulate and, therefore, very easy to follow. Yet that leaves no gray area, no room for discussion or debate, and there is nothing Jewish about that whatsoever. Jews are not a people of the simple answer. Of 5,000 legal arguments begun in the Talmud, not more than fifty are settled on the page. So, too, go the arguments over sexual ethics in relationships: There is a great deal to discuss.

It is easy with this case study to flash back to the seventh grade, in which all communication about relationships, romantic or otherwise, happened through peer pressure, triangulation, intermediaries, neglect, or acts of hallway violence. In the context of sexual relationships, making assumptions—deciding what someone else must be thinking without doing anything foolish like *asking* them about it—was more dangerous than even chemistry lab.

But once we get past seventh grade, we begin to develop better communication skills (even if we may still resort to slamming doors from time to time). And sexual relationships are the perfect place to exercise these skills for our benefit and pleasure. There is no reason to assume anything about the rules in a relationship—you get to make them as you go. It is up to you to decide when Seeing Each Other becomes Dating, and what that may mean, and when words like "boyfriend" or "girlfriend" may get used, and what *that* means. You, and your partner or partners, may and should choose modes of relating sexually that are clearly communicated and that serve your personal sexual ethics.

In a perfect world, all of the questions posed in this case study have the same answer: it depends on what the people involved have agreed upon. And yet the questions, as presented, suggest that no prior communication about the ethics of the individuals or their relationships has taken place. This is the crux of the problem. The words "assume" and "presume" are almost never useful in relationship communication, and nowhere less so than in sexual relationships. While one might easily be forgiven for assuming that his/her beloved would also enjoy a garlic bagel with peanut butter, the forgiveness for, "I just assumed it was okay to make out with someone else as long as we didn't have sex," is likely to be slower in coming (leaving aside entirely the conversation about what, exactly, constitutes having had sex).

At the risk of sounding more like Miss Manners than a scholar of sexuality, those in relationships that are not long enough in duration or sufficient in closeness to warrant a long and tender conversation about everyone's wants and needs regarding romantic or sexual exclusivity have no business presuming anything about anyone. If you are giving your body, your heart, or both to someone else, you are engaging in a very intimate, very specific behavior (even if very briefly). Deciding upon the boundaries of something as amorphous as a relationship based only on what you think and without any discussion with your partner about what he or she thinks is not a good plan.

Because of this, sexual ethics demands that we forgive partners any transgressions of social assumptions to which they have not explicitly agreed. This isn't to say you're not justified in ending a relationship if your partner does not subscribe to the same social values that you do. That is a perfectly good reason to break up. But you must understand that you are breaking up because your values differ, not because she or he was a cheating scoundrel, and you must represent the circumstances appropriately to others if asked. It's not possible to break an agreement (which is what cheating means) where no agreement has been made.

The good news about this is that well-communicated, non-coercive agreements between partners about sex, when enacted as agreed upon, have the bonus of being almost ethically unimpeachable. If Pat and Sam had talked about their relationship and been able to agree that, for example, they were very attracted to each other but unsure that the relationship was ready for sexual exclusivity, then they could have decided what their rules would be for other-dating or for sex. Pat's date with Alex would, in these circumstances, be perfectly ethical. If, on the other hand, Pat and Sam had agreed that they would date each other exclusively, then Pat and Alex's date would become unethical. Likewise with Alex and Sam. However difficult it may be to confess an outside attraction or an interest in an extracurricular date—and it certainly can be—that conversation also serves an important purpose. If the new prospect is so appealing that it makes the difficult talk seem worth having, then this too may be revealing. If one is not reasonably sure that a new date or lover is serious or interesting enough to warrant conversation about him/her with one's current date or lover, maybe it's better to skip both the talk and the date.

It is also possible that Pat and Sam's agreement could allow for sex or sexual play with others, but in ways in which they both feel comfortable, without creating emotional intimacy outside the relationship. Or that Jamie and Alex's agreement could allow for up to three dates with a potential new partner before it would be time to talk about what it all means. Polyamory, a word that means "many loves," is the organizing principle behind many relationships, and within this context it is considered entirely appropriate to pursue new intimate partners within the parameters of a couple's agreement. This might include, for example, having sex with others, but only as part of a threesome with or in the presence of one's partner; dating other women but not men (or vice versa); having sexual partners while traveling but not at home; reserving certain sexual activities for each other; and so forth. All of these agreements are ethically sound ways to arrange a relationship of any duration.

But let us now wade into more complicated waters. Suppose that Pat and Sam had agreed that they would be sexually monogamous, and made no provision for window-shopping, and then Pat accepted Alex's invitation. Knowing that there is some sexual chemistry between Pat and Alex, a logical case could be made either way for disclosure or nondisclosure: Pat could tell because she or he is considering the possibility of sex with Alex, or could not tell because the date does not result in sexual activity. But ethics, which demands of not just the brain but also of the heart and soul, say that for Pat to keep silent in this case would be to make an excuse built on *pilpul* (empty analysis), and would not be faithful to the agreement with Sam.

What's more, in this instance, Pat would be acting unethically not only to Sam but also to Alex, by making Alex an unwitting party to an unethical date. As with many other things in a sexual context, sexual ethics are transitive. Assuming that there is an agreement for sexual exclusivity and no explicit rules allowing trying-before-buying, it would be as odious an ethical transgression for Pat to accept Alex's invitation without telling Alex of his/her agreement with Sam as it would be for Pat to accept without telling Sam about it. It would be a double violation of trust.

25

And what about the conversations in these agreements? Good, ethical communication and decision making about the ethos of a relationship is free of power dynamics, control, and coercion. It is fair to say, "I cannot be in a relationship with someone who wants to be sexual with others," but not to say, "You look like a Nice Jewish Boy, but you're really a slut." Likewise, it is fair to say, "I would prefer an arrangement where we can have other relationships, but not just random sex," but, "Do you really think you can satisfy all my emotional needs while you obsess about your garden?" is a non-starter.

People raised in American culture are, by and large, already loaded up with a giant dose of shame and silence about sex and sexuality. There's no point making it worse, and no point in judging. If your partner, or potential partner, wants an arrangement that you don't, whether in sexual expression or in living room furniture, you are certainly not obliged to accept the terms. However, neither can you deride him or her for his or her desires if those desires are being discussed as you're creating a relationship agreement. You may also want to consider the potential long-term value of someone who is self-aware and self-confident enough to consider and discuss honestly what she or he wants and how she or he sees a relationship working.

While all the problems with our media-saturated culture are greater than the scope of this essay, the most relevant one isn't: the way that the media portrays relationship progression. Movies, which are more than happy to show graphic scenes of sexuality, shy away from graphic scenes of relationship communication in the same way that pornographic movies never show the use of sexual lubricants. Both of these cinematic omissions, which are designed to simplify interaction, produce the same dangerous effect: they contribute to the erroneous and unhealthy idea that these steps can be skipped when they cannot (or at least, not without the potential for significant pain), and they further the questionable premise that skipping the sticky part makes it magically disappear. This is not so.

Movies that show the "spontaneous" sexual encounter, followed by blissful relationship happiness, somehow manage to leave out the "So, what are we doing here?" conversation, unless they can play it for laughs or dramatic value. They do not show the breakfast, two weeks later, where someone summons the courage to say, awkwardly, "So ... Simone asked me today if you were my girlfriend now, and I, uh, wasn't sure what to say."

This is a shame, because as anyone in a long-term relationship will tell you, great sex, while it has substantial value, is even still not more important to a relationship than great communication. The pernicious media-culture habit of making these difficult conversations invisible contributes to the idea that they're not necessary. And it supports the fallacy that if people are really, *really* in love, they will magically have all the same values, all the same wants and needs, and will effortlessly intuit the other's desires about intimacy and commitment, which will naturally be a perfect match.

This case study—and, in fact, a great deal of Jewish law—is concerned with obligation. In the realm of sexual ethics, the primary obligation is honest communication and the creation of a mutually agreeable arrangement. You do not have to agree. You do not have to stay in the relationship. You do not have to change your mind or heart if you do not agree. You do not have to have more or less sexual freedom than you had wanted or counted on. But sexual ethics demands that you make yourself willing to talk about who may do what with whom and under what circumstances, and with what notice or lack thereof. And, furthermore, if you find yourself unable to sit down and have that conversation, sexual ethics demands you not lie down with anyone until you can.

Holy Uncertainty: Judaism and Dating

Scott Perlo

I'M A RABBI, so I'm used to considering the major questions of life through what our Tradition has to say on the topic. However, our Rabbis, may their memory be for a blessing, didn't do much dating themselves—the whole idea of courtship didn't really exist until the 1830s, and dating with the possibility of sex certainly wasn't socially acceptable until the second half of the 20th century. Accordingly, the amount of explicit Jewish material available on dating, other than exhortations not to do it, is miniscule. This doesn't mean that Judaism has little to say about dating—our Tradition is flexible in the most elegant sense—just that it's not always clear where to look for what it says.

Furthermore, the word "dating" in its broadest sense can encompass multiple types of relationships, from years of monogamy to one-night stands. The ethics of each of these relationships is governed, to my mind, primarily by the assumptions that each partner brings to the table, and those assumptions can be radically different throughout our culture, from monogamy starting on date one to monogamy never. Dating isn't one thing, it is many, and its definition differs on almost a person-to-person basis.

It's hard to write about dating, hard to say something of some depth in a Jewish context without some real work. So I'm going to begin by addressing what I think dating is not and then using what I've learned from that process of elimination to describe what dating is.

Dating Is Not Marriage

My biggest frustration is that most rabbis speak about dating as some kind of miniature version of marriage, with all the same rules applying, just slightly less so. I would never argue that they're not like each other, but the differences between dating and marriage are also crucially important.

To simplify, marriage is about the combination of commitment and sex. Marriage has within it the agreement that the two parties will commit to each other against all odds and preserve the marriage with every resource that they can muster. That commitment should be so strong that it can persist even after adultery; there is a long tradition of helping partners to mend a relationship after such betrayal. This isn't to say that marriages are forever—divorce is an option in Jewish law for a reason—but that the intention from the beginning is that the marriage last the entire lifespan of one of the spouses.

Commitment in a marriage extends beyond the emotions and selves of the two partners. That is to say, marriage is also a commitment that usually involves joining two families together and two bank accounts into one, living together, the legal recognition of two people as a single unit, and plenty of other emotional and logistical transitions.

Moreover, marriages are, in Jewish thought, necessarily about sex (and about children, according to our sources). In fact, Jewish law originally stipulated that having sex actually enacts marriage when it's paired with the specific intention to do so by both partners (and witnesses, which is a discussion for another essay). Our Rabbis weren't thrilled about this form of enactment, but nonetheless continually recognized it as being possible. In addition, holding out on sex for longer than a week against the will of one of the partners was deemed grounds for ending a marriage. And I think that we, even living in this modern world with all of its possibilities, would agree with this principle, for who would regard a marriage devoid of sex as healthy?

Dating is not marriage. Dating is not necessarily tied to sex, and even though most dating in the liberal world includes sex, it certainly isn't an obligation. There is nothing aberrant about couples either refraining from sex entirely or limiting it in some way while they are dating.

And dating is not about commitment; it is about the *possibility* of commitment. Dating is, in most of its forms, about trying things out, about seeing whether both partners want to be committed to each other. To do that we engage in a limited form of commitment, most often sexual and emotional, sometimes financial (traveling together, living together for some couples), to see whether or not we want to fully entwine our lives. However, this element of trying, waiting to see whether or not a person is the right match, profoundly distinguishes dating from marriage. In dating there is always the understanding, or fear, that a match may not work out, in which case the two people involved will go their separate ways without the years it takes to work out financial separation and custody situations.

So dating isn't marriage. It also isn't something for which there is a set playbook (would that it were so easy!). Instead, it is the chance to be intimately uncertain with another human being. Dating is about uncertainty, about learning to shepherd uncertainty and allowing it either to grow into a commitment or a separation. The question we need to ask, as a result, is how we embrace that uncertainty when we're in relationships, and how we honor it while protecting both people involved. For this reason, I think that the gender and sexuality of the partners does not matter at all. The obligation to protect another human being and treat that person well has no gendered boundaries or boundaries of sexual orientation.

Holy Uncertainty

The question of how to embrace uncertainty is a very straightforward one. But the problem with straightforward questions is that the answers are often messy, nowhere more so than in relationships. So to try to answer this question, I want to bring in a metaphor from Torah.

One of the pleasant things about our Torah is that it doesn't have much patience for idealized relationships. There isn't a single one in the text that I can think of that isn't fraught with real tensions and a whole lot of problems. As a result, Torah can speak to both difficult relationships and difficulties in relationships with a relevance that is almost surprising. One moment in particular is of use for our purposes, an example of one of the failures in the relationship between God and Israel.

During our time in the desert we didn't eat food, per se. We ate manna, which was both quite good and easy to collect. No matter how much time one spent harvesting it, everyone would gather the same amount. The first question to ask, for the purposes of our metaphor, is why manna in the first place? It does not seem, from other biblical sources, that God had any concern about providing regular food. What was the point of the manna?

Here's the Torah's response: "And God said to Moshe, 'Behold, I will rain down bread for you from the sky, and the people shall go out and gather each day that day's portion—that I may test them, to see whether they will follow my instruction or not.'"[1]

There were definitely some who were not satisfied with the situation:

"The riffraff in their midst felt a gluttonous craving; and then the Israelites wept and said, 'If only we had meat to eat! We remember the fish that we used to eat free in Egypt, the cucumbers, the melons, the

---

1. Exodus 16:4.

leeks, the onions, and the garlic. Now our gullets are shriveled. There is nothing at all! Nothing but this manna to look to!'" (Num. 11:4–6)

God was not pleased with this complaint, and eventually fed the people so much meat that they choked on it.

So what was the problem? Why was the desire for variety such an anathema?

I understand manna as the symbol of the early romance between God and the Jewish people. Manna is both real and not real, like early infatuation. The thing about manna was that you didn't have to work for it; it existed in the same amount no matter how much you invested in collecting it, and it was meant to be replaced by the harvest once Israel made it into the Promised Land.[2] Manna hinted at the promise of a fuller relationship, one that was built on work and a mutual covenant, but one that had not yet been realized.

The Israelites couldn't figure this out. When the newness and novelty of the manna began to fade, they made a double mistake. First, they idealized their life before the covenant with God, "We remember the fish that we used to eat *free* in Egypt, the cucumbers, the melons, the leeks, the onions, and the garlic." This, of course, was ridiculous—the life of slavery that they endured had a high price, whether or not their slave masters required them to pay for their food. Second, they weren't able to realize what the manna represented—a honeymoon, as it were—and that the substance for which they were looking required a deeper commitment, not a lesser one.

As the mistake was doubled, so was the lesson: In order to protect our partners and ourselves, and in order to allow the possibilities to play out, we have to be able to be patient with the uncertainty of our relationships, be that expressed through boredom, infatuation, or doubt. Both idealizing other relationships and expecting more from a relationship we have than that connection is ready to provide are ways of being impatient with what we've got, as the Israelites were impatient with manna.

Creating Ethics for Relationships

The Ben Ish Ḥai, the brilliant leader of Baghdadi Jewry at the beginning of the 20th century, was once sent a question regarding lying. There's a verse

---

2. Deuteronomy 25.

from the Torah that commands, "Keep far from a false charge ...."[3] This is understood to be a broad and very stringent prohibition against lying. However, there are a number of specific instances in which the Torah commands lying, including cases in which peace can be preserved or embarrassment can be prevented.[4] Knowing this, the questioners asked the Ben Ish Ḥai to resolve the contradictions for them, so that they could know in which cases lying was permitted, even obligatory, and when it was forbidden.

To this, the Ben Ish Ḥai wrote, "I am not going to give you the inventions of my own mind as to the situations in which there is permission in this matter. I will only bring you the situations listed in the Talmud, and you should learn from them ...." The list of situations where lying may be permitted was 12 pages long.

His decision not to tell his questioners what to do is very unusual. What he seems to be saying is that there are no overarching rules that he can give. It isn't that he thinks that it's impossible to be guilty of the sin of lying, nor that truth and lies are in the eye of the beholder, but that knowing whether or not a lie is allowed or needed always depends upon the situation. There are, quite simply, no hard and fast rules. The need to lie, or the demand to tell the truth, is contextual.

I believe that the same thing is true for dating: there's no formula for knowing what is right and what is wrong. This by no means indicates that there isn't such a thing as right or wrong, but that the definitions of fidelity and betrayal, obligation and permission depend upon the specific relationship.

Here's why: whether people perceive the boundaries of their relationship as being preserved or broken depends on what they think the boundaries of the given relationship are. That thinking comes from a whole bevy of sources: individual psyches, cultural assumptions, family patterns, past experiences, etc. Most people aren't explicitly aware that what they think are assumptions. They're more likely to understand their requirements as just the way relationships are. When you multiply those assumptions by two people, a lot of misunderstanding can result.

---

3. Exodus 23:7.
4. Babylonian Talmud, *Yevamot* 65b. The rabbis also used to lie when asked about their learning (as a measure of humility) or about their sex lives (as a measure of modesty), or when asked if someone else's hospitality was particularly excellent (so that masses of people would not take advantage of a good host), Babylonian Talmud, *Bava Metzi'a* 23b. See also Babylonian Talmud, *Berakhot* 27b.

The same is true for successful marriages, to some degree. However, marriage is, in this case, distinguished from dating because, Jewishly speaking, marriage has fixed rules: for example, don't cheat on your spouse.[5] But in dating, partners first need to agree upon or assume exclusivity before infidelity can exist. First dates don't constitute contracts.

Moreover, we should know where we are in relationships, to the best of our ability. This isn't the same thing as knowing where we're going, an expectation that can kill a connection before it has come to fruition. Rather, we have to find out what our expectations are of each other, and revisit them quite often as those expectations grow and develop. We have to talk about what we need.

Patience and honesty aren't quick remedies to what ails relationships, but they have the advantages of being true and heartfelt virtues. We should have patience for our partners. We should be as honest with them as we're able to be without hurting them. I have faith that where we can accomplish these virtues, and when the connection is ready, love will grow:

I adjure you, O maidens of Jerusalem,
By gazelles or by hinds of the field:
Do not wake or rouse
Love until it please! (Songs 3:5)

---

5. There are, of course, some fixed rules that apply to dating, but these rules apply regardless of whether the two people involved have a relationship, and usually fall under the category of the law; for example, the rule of not abusing your partner, sexually, physically, or otherwise.

CASE 2

⁜

SEXUAL CONSEQUENCES

Case Study

R ACHEL AND MATT, both in their early 20s, are sexually involved. If their relationship is a one-night stand, what obligations does each partner have to use contraceptive devices? What if they're in a sexual relationship that has gone on for one month? What if they're in a sexual relationship that has been monogamous for six months?

If Rachel suspected that their birth control methods were not effective (a broken condom, a missed birth control pill, etc.), should she take the "morning after pill," known as Mifeprex (mifeprestone) or RU-486? If she has not used RU-486 and is further along in a pregnancy, for what reasons might she consider abortion? Does she have an obligation to inform Matt? If so, when? If their relationship is a one-night stand? One month? Six months? Does she have an obligation to take his wishes into consideration if their relationship is a one-night stand? One month? Six months?

Do you have a right not to be tested for STDs if you are sexually active? If you have tested positive for an STD, under what circumstances are you obligated to inform your next partner? Under what circumstances are you not required to do so? Given that some STDs are lethal, and that some pose health issues that may be painful or uncomfortable but are not lethal, and that some are curable and some are not, does the nature of the STD make a difference in your obligations? If you test positive for an STD, are you required to inform previous partners? If you're not sure where you contracted the STD, how far back in your dating history should you go to inform people? Does the nature of the STD affect that obligation?

At what age should people be taught about safe sex? At what age should they be taught about communicating with their partners about safe sex? Is abstinence-only education justifiable?

Traditional Sources

Compiled by Uzi Weingarten and the Editors

On Birth Control

1. Babylonian Talmud, *Yevamot* 12b

Rabbi Bebai recited before Rabbi Nahman: There are three classes of women who employ an absorbent [for purposes of contraception]: a minor, a pregnant woman, and a nursing mother: a minor lest she become pregnant and die, a pregnant woman lest miscarriage result, and a nursing mother lest she become pregnant and prematurely wean the child so that it dies. And what is a minor? From the age of eleven years and a day until the age of twelve years and a day. One who is under or over this age carries on her marital intercourse in the usual manner—so says Rabbi Meir. But the other Sages say: The one as well as the other carries on her marital intercourse in the usual manner, and mercy be vouchsafed from Heaven, for [Scripture says in Psalms 116:6], "The Lord preserves the simple."

Note: The Talmud speaks of two modes through which contraception was attempted: a sponge (*mokh*) inserted in the vaginal canal to absorb sperm before it got to the uterus, and "a cup of roots" (*kos ikarin*), presumably an oral potion that was thought to prevent conception.

2. Elliot N. Dorff, *Matters of Life and Death: A Jewish Approach to Modern Medical Ethics* (Philadelphia: The Jewish Publication Society, 1998), 122–123

As a matter of course, the law follows the majority opinion, in this case that of the Sages. But what are they saying? The Hebrew text uses the present tense, indicative verb in the first clause, as the translation, "employ," indicates. If that verb is taken to mean that there are three classes of women who *may* use a contraceptive device, the implication would be that other women may not, even according to Rabbi Meir. With that understanding, the Sages would not even permit the three classes of women to use contraception despite the fact that their health or that of their fetus or baby is at stake. Later rabbis who adopt this reasoning, however, permit contraception to preserve the woman's life or health; they then apply the prohibition of contraception embedded in this source exclusively to cases where the woman will incur only a minor elevation of risk beyond that of normal pregnancy if she becomes pregnant.

If, on the other hand, the operative verb in the above quotation is interpreted to mean that there are three classes of women who *should* or *must* use an absorbent, the implication would be that while these women are obligated to use a contraceptive device in order to protect their health or that of their fetus or baby, other women may use contraceptive devices for other purposes as well. Those other purposes may then be strictly or leniently defined.

On Abortion

3. Exodus 21:22–23

When men fight, and one of them pushes a pregnant woman and a miscarriage results, but no other damage ensues, the one responsible shall be fined according as the woman's husband may exact from him, the payment to be as the judges determine. But if other damage ensues, the penalty shall be life for life.

4. Mishnah, *Arakhin* 1:4

A woman who left [the court] to be executed, we do not wait for her to give birth. If she sat on the birthing stool, we wait till she gives birth.

5. Maimonides (Rambam), *Mishneh Torah*, Laws of Courts 12:4, based on the Babylonian Talmud, *Arakhin* 7a

The reason for that is that we do not "delay justice" by postponing the execution. Not only do we not wait for a pregnant woman to give birth, but the fetus is actually killed first.

6. Mishnah, *Ohalot* 7:6

[If] a woman [is] struggling to deliver, they [should] cut up the fetus in her womb and remove it limb by limb, because her life (Hebrew, *hayehah*) has priority over the fetus's life. If most of the fetus has been delivered, they may not touch it, because we do not override one life (Hebrew, *nefesh*) for another.

7. Maimonides (Rambam), *Mishneh Torah*, Laws of Murder 1:9, based on the Babylonian Talmud, *Sanhedrin* 72b

The Sages therefore taught that [if] a pregnant woman is struggling to deliver, one may cut up the fetus in her womb, whether using a potion or by hand, because he is like a pursuer (*rodef*) coming to kill her. Once its head has been delivered, one may not injure the fetus, for we do not override one life for another, and this is the way of the world.

8. Maimonides, *Mishneh Torah*, Laws of Heave Offerings 8:3, based on the Babylonian Talmud, *Yevamot* 69b

For the first forty days it is not a fetus but rather ordinary water.

On the Duty to Avoid Danger
9. Deuteronomy 22:8

When you build a new house, you shall make a parapet for your roof, so that you do not bring bloodguilt on your house if anyone should fall from it.

10. Maimonides, *Mishneh Torah*, Laws of Murder 11:4–5

4. So too with regard to any danger that threatens life, it is a positive commandment to remove it and [thereby] to avoid [the danger] and to be very careful in this matter, for it is written: 'Be careful and guard your life' (Deuteronomy 4:9). If one does not remove [the danger] and leaves standing those dangers that threaten life, one violates this commandment and transgresses "Do not bring bloodshed in your house" (Deuteronomy 22:8).

5. There are many things that the Sages prohibited because they can be life-threatening. And whoever says, "I will take my chances, and it is not anybody's business," or "I am not concerned about this [danger]" is flogged.

11. Babylonian Talmud, *Hullin* 10a

Avoiding danger is more incumbent on us than avoiding any of the other prohibitions of the Torah.

Contemporary Sources

Compiled by Steven Edelman-Blank

On Birth Control and Sexually Transmitted Diseases
1. Leah Furman, *Single Jewish Female: A Modern Guide to Sex and Dating* (New York: Perigee, 2004), 126

Men have been interpreting the terms in the Torah to suit their own needs for centuries. If you are not bound by the rules of religious convention and would like to do the same, focus on the emphasis that the Torah puts on protecting human life. Your life.

If premarital sex is on the agenda, be careful. Put your health above all else and use condoms to avoid AIDS and other sexually transmitted diseases. If you don't like the effect that birth control pills have on your body, by all means, don't use them. Just make sure you're protected. In Judaism, as in life, your survival is the highest priority.

2. Ruth K. Westheimer and Jonathan Mark. *Heavenly Sex: Sexuality in the Jewish Tradition* (New York: New York University Press, 1995), 59

Safe sex and sacred sex are not opposite but complementary. A lover, attempting to live a life in accord with God as well as his or her love partner, will, for example, be honest and caring to avoid the spread of disease. Here, the heart, soul, and brain are as important as the penis or the vagina.

3. Michael Gold, *Does God Belong in the Bedroom?* (Philadelphia: The Jewish Publication Society, 1992), 110–111

For single people who are sexually active, it is patently irresponsible not to use birth control. In fact, from a Jewish point of view, such usage is more vital for them than for married couples. A married couple may find an accidental pregnancy to be untimely, and it may even create a family crisis, but such a pregnancy does not break with the norms of Jewish marriage.

For a single woman, an unplanned pregnancy raises numerous difficult issues of Jewish law and morality....

Given these realities, unmarried people who engage in sexual activity, including young people, must have access to birth control information. The same hierarchy of Jewish values would govern their use. A woman's use of contraceptives would be more acceptable than a man's, and the method that caused the least interference with the enjoyment of the sex act is preferred.

4. Elliot N. Dorff. *Love Your Neighbor and Yourself: A Jewish Approach to Modern Personal Ethics* (Philadelphia: The Jewish Publication Society, 2003), 115–116

It is, therefore, imperative to recognize that sexual contact with *any* new partner raises the possible risk of contracting sexually transmitted diseases, including lethal ones. Not only is that a pragmatic word to the wise but it comes out of the depths of the Jewish moral and legal tradition, where *pikuah nefesh* (saving a life) is a value of the highest order. Moreover we are commanded by our tradition to take measures to prevent illness in the first place.

5. **Louanne Cole Weston, "When and How to Reveal You Have an STD,"** ***WebMD the Magazine*** **(2007). Available at http://www.webmd.com/ sexual-conditions/features/when-how-reveal-you-have-std**

Opening up about an STD (particularly the ones that you cannot "cure," like HPV, HIV, and herpes) can be intimidating, whether you're 20-something or 50-something. You might wonder: Why risk rejection? I'm safe if I always use a condom or avoid sex whenever I have an outbreak, right?

In a word: no. It's not always possible to know with complete certainty when an STD like herpes is transmissible ....

Timing is everything. Gather information on your STD, since your intended sexual partner may have questions. Your attitude and mood will influence how your disclosure is received, so broach the topic when you are relaxed and can devote your full attention to the conversation. Do it in a private place, but not en route to a romantic weekend. Nor should such a discussion happen in the midst of a passionate embrace. That's a mood killer and can lead to an angry response by your partner.

6. **Ruth K. Westheimer with Pierre A. Lehu, *Sex for Dummies*, 3rd edition (Hoboken, NJ: Wiley Publishing, 2007), 273**

You all know the Golden Rule about doing onto others as you would have them do unto you. If you planned to have sex with someone, and they had a sexually transmitted disease, wouldn't you want them to tell you in advance? The same applies to you: If you have a sexually transmitted disease, you have to tell any potential partners. Notice that I said potential because I won't hide the fact that, if you tell somebody that you have an STD, that person may suddenly run in the opposite direction. If you have a disease, such as herpes, which never goes away, you will face not only a lifetime of outbreaks, but also difficulty in finding partners. You have to accept that. You cannot go around infecting other people.

On Abortion

7. Daniel Schiff, *Abortion in Judaism* (Cambridge, United Kingdom: Cambridge University Press, 2002), 227–228

Among the few observations that may be made with certainty concerning Judaism and abortion is that, in its practical rulings, Jewish law has usually eschewed extreme positions. This outcome was not strategically planned in order to make Jewish views more palatable to external critics. Polarized positions on abortion are, after all, normative within contemporary society. There are outlooks that advocate that abortion should always be prohibited, even if it is to save the life of the mother. Conversely, there are standpoints that express precisely the opposite: that a woman's decision to have an abortion ought to be accepted, no matter what her reason for desiring the procedure. As the rabbis have demonstrated, however, the Jewish consensus views on abortion do not accord with either of these approaches. Rather, normative *halakhic* positions have always held that some amount of abortion is required—in order to save the life of the mother—but have uniformly rejected abortions that cannot be justified either because of maternal need, or for a threat to the fetus, or perhaps to save another child. In reality, however, while this more centrist position has much to commend it, it also has proven to be somewhat unfocused: more extreme stances have a clarity that is difficult to maintain closer to midstream.

8. "Reform Movement Applauds FDA's Long-Awaited Approval of So-Called 'Abortion Pill'," Religious Action Center of Reform Judaism. Available at http://rac.org/Articles/index.cfm?id=817&pge_prg_id=10214

WASHINGTON, September 29, 2000—Rabbi David Saperstein, Director of the Religious Action Center of Reform Judaism, responded to yesterday's announcement that the FDA had approved Mifepristone with the following statement:

> By approving Mifepristone (known in France as RU-486), the FDA has successfully placed women's fertility back in the hands of a woman and her doctor. The Reform movement of Judaism has long supported a woman's right to make moral decisions about her own life and her own body with privacy and without fear of government intrusion.

9. **Francesca Lunzer Kritz, "Jewish Law and RU-486," *The Jewish Journal*, October 26, 2000. Available at http://www.jewishjournal. com/health/article/jewish_law_and_ru_486_20001027/**

Rabbi Moshe Tendler, considered the leading Orthodox authority on Jewish medical ethics, and a professor at Yeshiva University… says that Mifeprex must be viewed in the context of what Jewish law says about abortion, which is that abortion is permitted only when a pregnancy places the mother's life in danger, and in consultation with a rabbinical authority…

But Tendler is significantly concerned that Mifeprex will be viewed as a form of contraception—"it is much easier to take a few pills a few days after you become pregnant than to take a pill every day in order to avoid a pregnancy," Tendler says. But that, he says, is halachically impermissible. "Contraception per se is not a free ride when it comes to Jewish law," Tendler says. "Not for married folk and certainly not for unmarried folk."

On Sex Education

10. **The United Synagogue of Conservative Judaism, "Comprehensive Sex Education 2007" Convention Resolution. Available at http://www.uscj.org/Sex_Education7473.html**

THEREFORE, BE IT RESOLVED that United Synagogue supports comprehensive sex education;

- Encourages parents to talk to their children about sexuality and sexual health in a Conservative Jewish context;
- Calls upon the U.S. Congress to cease funding of abstinence-only education;
- Opposes funding of abstinence-only education on federal, state, provincial and local levels;
- Encourages the support of the inclusion of components of age-appropriate comprehensive sex education in public schools; and
- Encourages components of age-appropriate comprehensive sex education in Solomon Schechter schools, Camps Ramah, Kadima, USY and Koach.

BE IT FURTHER RESOLVED that United Synagogue will develop age-appropriate educational materials to be used in day schools, synagogue schools, youth groups and homes.

11. **Avraham Peretz Friedman, *Marital Intimacy: A Traditional Jewish Approach* (Northvale, New Jersey: Jason Aronson, Inc, 1996), 4**

We have an obligation to our children to teach them Torah values in all matters, not least of all this one, early on, before they are exposed to foreign, destructive ideas, in accordance with the principal that whatever comes in first makes the deepest impression. Bad attitudes learned because of our neglect will color and distort irreparably our children's attitudes to marital intimacy for a lifetime. One of the greatest gifts we can give our children is a clear-eyed, holy vision of marital intimacy, untainted by the corrupted, perverse notions of the non-Torah world.

12. **Jewish Council for Public Affairs, "Task Force Concern on Comprehensive Sexuality Education in Public Schools Adopted By The 2008 JCPA Plenum." Available at http://www.jewishpublicaffairs.org/organizations. php3?action=printContentTypeHome&orgid=54&typeID=163**

The JCPA believes that public schools have an obligation to provide young people with accurate and effective sexuality education and, therefore, that current, ineffective abstinence-only-until-marriage sexuality programs in public schools should be replaced by comprehensive, medically accurate, age-appropriate sexuality education that does not promote any particular religious viewpoint on sexuality.

Responses

Building a Framework for Sexual Decision Making
Gloria Feldt

Let him give me of the kisses of his mouth!
For your love is more delightful than wine. (Songs 1:2)

A S THESE deliciously sensual lines imply, when it comes to sex and the expression of sexuality, we are fortunate as Jews to see intimacy through a framework in which sexuality is a positive element of our human nature. Sexual pleasure is even considered a mitzvah, to be celebrated whether for procreation or pleasure or both simultaneously.

We are fortunate to have a religious framework that does not taint such a beautiful thing as sex with the inherency of evil stemming from original sin. And as a woman, I am glad to be part of a religious tradition that insists that I have as much right to sexual satisfaction as a man, and one that also values my life when it comes to making a choice about whether to continue a pregnancy. Further, public opinion polls tell us that in the secular world, Jews top the charts in our socio-political support for access to birth control and legal abortion. Almost 90% of American Jews identify as pro-choice as compared to less than 60% of non-Jews.[1]

But none of this means we are or should be sexual libertines. For there is hardly an area of human behavior more fraught with tension between the temporal and the ethereal than that of sex and intimacy.

Sustain me with raisin cakes,
Refresh me with apples,
For I am faint with love. (Songs 2:5)

Sexual decisions require so many choices that affect ourselves and others. And because these decisions are so often made during the heat of passion, even the most rational among us can find our judgment clouded by what our bodies want to do when we are "faint with love" in the moment.

---

1. Michael Paulsen, "The Spiritual Life: Jews See US as Secular, Survey Says," *The Boston Globe*, July 15, 2000. Available at http://www.cjcs.net/press.htm#bg.

A Social Justice Framework for Sexual Decisions and Actions

Let me start with this social justice framework:

Equality between partners is the first and most necessary condition to achieving fully voluntary, non-coerced, and mutually pleasurable sexual relations, into which both partners can enter with a whole heart and mutual respect.

Neither Jews nor Jewish religion and culture are immune from the sexism and heterosexism that underlie many of society's negative attitudes about sex. Peel back the layers on the question of the nature and purpose of sexuality, and you will inevitably find that the debate is really about women's roles. In short, it's about who controls the means of reproduction and, by extension, the means of attaining wealth and social power. Gender injustices abound within traditional Jewish liturgy, starting with the daily prayer thanking God that the (assumed male) supplicant wasn't born a woman. Rabbi Arthur Waskow observes that one of the main pillars of traditional Jewish sexual ethics is the assumption that men rule over women in each household as they do in the society at large. Men are to act graciously and please women (sexually, economically, etc.)—but from a position of power. Clearly, the patriarchy is alive and well and so deeply embedded in so much of our thinking that it easily goes unnoticed when it is not specifically articulated.

So this business of judging individual sexual behavior can seem rather messy, and the tendency is to default either to the safety of rigid religious dictates or to take a rigidly scientific, public health approach that focuses on prevention of disease and unintended pregnancy to the exclusion of the very real concerns that make sexual decisions multilayered—emotional ("Is this love or lust?"), practical ("What will we do if she becomes pregnant?"), and ethical ("What is the right thing to do in a complicated circumstance?").

The answers are easy for the very traditional, who simply say "no" to sex outside of marriage and even restrict and set specific rules for sex within marriage. But let's be real: most people, even those who purport to be traditional, do not live by such rigid structures. In fact, most people, regardless of persuasion, begin having sexual relations in their mid-to-late teenage years, and around 90% have intercourse prior to marriage.[2]

---

2. "Premarital Sex Is Nearly Universal Among Americans, and Has Been for Decades," Guttmacher Institute, Dec. 19, 2006. Available at http://www.guttmacher.org/media/nr/2006/12/19/index.html

This does not represent moral decline, as fundamentalists are inclined to allege. In modern society, with an economy requiring significant educational attainment and work experience before people can support a family, most of us have 10 to 20 years between puberty and marriage. Celibacy during that time is possible but not likely. I doubt that is the sanest or healthiest way to live, and even though many see it as the ideal, it's an ideal that few live up to.

In any case, whether celibate or sexually involved with others, we humans have no choice but to make choices. And the hardest truth to embrace is that we are responsible to ourselves and to others for the consequences of our individual choices about sex and intimacy.

The Principles of the Social Justice Framework

Let us go early to the vineyards;
Let us see if the vine has flowered,
If its blossoms have opened,
If the pomegranates are in bloom.
There I will give my love to you. (Songs 7:13)

If we put down firm roots in a social justice framework, then taking on the responsibility of making choices that restrain and balance our sexual activity might not be so difficult. If our social justice imperative as human beings and as Jews is to repair the world, then with equality and mutuality as the framework, the following four principles can guide our decisions on sex, relationships, sexual health, and childbearing:

- The Whole Heart Test: Do you feel reluctant to enter this particular relationship or participate in this particular sexual act? If so, then don't. It probably doesn't fit the social justice framework, either because there is a power imbalance between the partners or because for some other reason it does not offer healing or equality.

- Respect for ourselves: We have an obligation to keep ourselves healthy and to protect ourselves from disease and other physical or emotional harm. We have an obligation to consider our own pleasure, life goals, and immediate capability to sustain a relationship. So will you still love yourself in the morning?

- Respect for others: We have an obligation not to cause deliberate harm to others, not to coerce or harass, not to lie or misrepresent our intentions, not to value our own pleasure over others' pleasure or health. Put more affirmatively, we have the same obligation to our partner's pleasure and mental and physical health as to our own. Would you want your partner to do this to you?

- Responsibility for our choices: Choice is the basis of morality. We are shaped by the choices we make as much as we shape them. Choice engenders sacrifice as well as freedom. We are responsible for the consequences of our decisions, including their effects on others, whether they be the offspring that may come from sexual relations, our partners or family members, or the community. Are you prepared to take responsibility for what you are about to/want to do?

Applying the Social Justice Framework to Rachel and Matt

But how do these fine social principles of the whole heart, respect for self and others, and responsibility apply to real life situations such as Rachel and Matt's?

As Tamara Kreinin, former president of SIECUS, a national sex education organization, says, "I think straight up they have to use protection from pregnancy and sexually transmitted infections unless, as in the case of pregnancy, otherwise discussed. If they get an HIV test right away and then another in six months and agree to be monogamous and they trust each other, then they could stop using condoms at that point. Though I must say I think that it is unlikely all those requirements will be met. For 20-year-olds, a three-month long relationship is 'long.'"

Judith Steinhart, a sex educator who founded Columbia University's sex information website Go Ask Alice! (http://www.goaskalice. columbia.edu/, which I highly recommend as a resource), says the same rules apply whether the relationship has lasted one day, six months, or longer, and regardless of the age of the individuals involved. If pregnancy is not wanted, she tells people to consider options for giving and receiving sexual pleasure that do not necessarily involve intercourse. This is also a viable option for observant men and women who want to "play by the rules." Steinhart says, "Rachel and Matt can make decisions about the kind of sex they want to have. Perhaps they are 'sexually involved' without intercourse, but with mutual touching to orgasm ... It's possible that they made a choice together, even for a one-night stand, to have mutual oral sex, and no penetration. In these scenarios, neither partner has to use contraceptive devices because the kind of sex they have is clearly for giving and receiving pleasure, even with meaning and connection. They are having recreational, even meaningful, but not procreational sex."

So those are the practical considerations. Before they get to that point, Rachel and Matt have a responsibility to ask themselves whether they feel ready to have sex with a whole heart. If the answer is "yes," and that applies whether they are contemplating a brief or longer-term relationship, then they must spend some time communicating openly and honestly with one another about their birth control and disease prevention methods before they hop into bed. And they might as well be prepared to discover that a brief sexual encounter is just not worth all the preparation and the discussion of some of life's most embarrassing aspects.

However, if Rachel suspects that she and Matt's birth control methods were not effective, should she take the morning after pill? If she is further along in a pregnancy, for what reasons might she consider abortion? Does she have an obligation to inform Matt if she decides to get one? If so, when? Does she have an obligation to take his wishes into consideration?

Emergency contraception, often called the "morning after pill," is backup contraception that Rachel should take as soon as possible, as it only works for 72 hours after intercourse. It is not abortion, and does not work if pregnancy has occurred (i.e., if the fertilized egg has implanted in the uterus). Many women keep a dose of emergency contraception in their medicine cabinet just in case of contraceptive failure. RU-486, or mifepristone as it is called in the U.S., is an early abortion pill. There is no difference in the moral sense between the decision to use mifepristone and the decision to have a surgical abortion, except in some instances in regard to the gestation of the pregnancy. As a matter of social justice, and certainly of equality for women, it is a fundamental human right to make one's own childbearing decisions, including the decision to carry a pregnancy to term or to have an abortion.

However, both partners should have a say in what to do about an unintended pregnancy. The website www.koshersex.com suggests there should be a "sliding scale" for sexual ethics in the modern world. For instance, the longer Rachel and Matt have been together, the closer of a relationship they have and thus the greater the obligation for her to speak with him about the pregnancy. That said, since only the woman carries a pregnancy at a risk to both her body and also her life plans, she alone must have the authority and the moral agency to make the final decision as to whether or not to carry a pregnancy to term.

But other issues come into play when you are in a sexually active relationship. For instance, do you have a right not to be tested for STDs? If you have tested positive for an STD, under what circumstances are you obligated to inform your partner? Also, when are you obligated to inform previous partners?

In keeping with respect for one's own body, we of course have the right not to accept an invasive procedure. But I would try to persuade Matt or Rachel that they show respect for their own bodies by getting tests that can protect their health and possibly protect their future fertility. Even some of the most common non-lethal STDs, such as chlamydia, can compromise one's fertility.

In addition, getting tested demonstrates respect for the other person who needs to know whether she or he has been exposed to an STD and needs medical attention—no one can escape responsibility here. If both agree to use a condom correctly, before and during the entire penetration, both partners are being responsible, but disclosure of a diagnosis is still essential. If the relationship has not been monogamous for a substantial length of time (six months is the timeframe for HIV, for example), then partners must think as though they have had sex with everyone their partners have had sex with and do their best to inform anyone who might be at risk of becoming infected.

Applying the Social Justice Framework to Sex Education
At what age should people be taught about safe sex and about communicating with their partners about safe sex? Is abstinence-only education justifiable? Ignorance is never bliss. Providing medically accurate information, along with a value system that encourages people to make healthy, responsible decisions about sex throughout their lifespan, is essential. Abstinence-only programs have now been demonstrated to be ineffective at best and harmful at worst. Young people in those programs are no less likely to become sexually active before marriage, but they are less likely to protect themselves and their partners from STDs and pregnancy when they do have sex.

All sex education should be age-appropriate. Explicit safe-sex communication techniques are generally taught beginning in middle school, with the level of explicitness and complexity increasing with age. However, teaching the fundamentals of equality, respect, and responsibility, and the principle of not doing anything or allowing anything to be done to you if it can't pass the whole heart test should begin as soon as

51

children start asking questions. This brings them to acknowledge the importance of taking responsibility for their sexual behavior.

As a cultural group, Jews have fewer unintended pregnancies, teen pregnancies, and abortions than most Americans of other faiths. This is in no small part because Judaism has a healthier, more realistic sexual ethic than the more conflicted one that pervades American culture. After all, the first step in making healthy, responsible decisions about sex and intimacy is being able to own and respect the sexual part of one's being and to respect it in one's partner. We therefore need to be clear-eyed about both the value of sex and its potential for causing problems, to put sex into a social justice framework that supports equality between partners, and to be able to say with a whole heart:

I am my beloved's and my beloved is mine. (Songs 6:3)

Making Meaning and Finding Morality in a Sexualized World

Deborah M. Roffman

LOOKING WORRIED and more than a little sad, a man spoke up at a workshop I led in San Francisco not long ago. A seasoned teacher in a private secular high school, he said, to nodding heads around the room, "I just can't figure out what yardsticks kids are using today to make decisions about sex. Truthfully, I'm really not sure they're using any."

Weeks later, I found myself with a group of sixth graders at a local Jewish day school. During the class, we discussed some of the possible consequences of sexual behavior, particularly sexual intercourse. Like most sixth graders, they were pretty knowledgeable about the physical ramifications—sexually transmitted diseases (STDs), pregnancy, and the like—but they knew almost nothing about the less concrete social and emotional implications (predictable in a group of preteens). I gave an example or two to prompt their thinking, and one of the girls suddenly seemed to get what I was talking about.

"Oh," she reported confidently, "my older cousin told me *exactly* what to do about *that*. She said you just decide not to become involved emotionally with the other person, and then you can't get hurt!"

The incident made me think of the man in San Francisco, and the resonance his comment had with the other educators and counselors present. This is it, I thought, just the kind of minimalist thinking he and the others were wondering and worrying about. If you reduce sexual behavior to just the physical mechanics, then there are no other aspects to measure, no other considerations to weigh, no yardsticks of any other kind to apply.

It is alarming to me how regularly I hear examples of sexual reductionism from my students—like the sixth grade boy who recently asked if it was correct that in middle school you *had* to have oral sex. Or the 11-year-old girl who stated as fact, since an older girl had told her, that it was important to have sexual experiences in middle school so you would be "good at it" by the time you were in high school. Or the older students I teach who think sex in some form with someone you just met is a good way to find out whether you should pursue a relationship.

It is impossible, and certainly unwise, to make hard and fast generalizations about young people and their sexual values and attitudes, particularly

53

based on anecdotal evidence. But, there seems to have been an unsettling shift in attitudes in recent years, particularly since the late 1990s.

Mass Media and Sexual Messages

It is tempting, and perhaps even justified, to blame "the media" for these changes. It now uses sex and gender stereotypes to sell *everything*—no longer just the standard beer, jeans, perfume, and popular entertainment fare, but such provocative and "sexy" items as tuna, refrigerators, floor tiles, hip and back surgery, and bathroom faucets (I have the ads to prove it). After all, how deeply rich and meaningful can sex be if it can be reduced to everything, and everything can be reduced to it?

Combined with this deliberate "dumbing down" of sex is an equally calculated dumbing down of adulthood that has also been promoted by marketers since the 1990s. Literally out of thin air, they have managed to manufacture a brand new demographic group—8- to 14-year-olds, or *Tweens*—a cynical and insidious marketing handle and a descriptor now used in everyday discourse. Having created a marketing bonanza by hawking adult-oriented, often sexually themed products to impressionable youngsters, advertisers now set their sites on children younger than eight, or *Teenies* (presumably young *Tweens*-in-training). The underlying message our children are being sold is the belief that sex is simple, in fact so simple that it is certainly simple enough for them, too. And many, apparently, are buying both the merchandise and the worldview that go along with it.

Many parents I know are dismayed and even panicked by the culture in which their children are being raised. They are disgusted by the fact that popular culture teaches values that are *directly opposite* to those they want their children to hold, yet many parents do not understand their role in either creating the problem or fixing it. For generations, families and schools have created a vacuum in children's lives around the topic of sexuality. In recent years, filling that void has been a virtual cakewalk for the entertainment, advertising, and merchandizing industries.

The Missing Discourse about Sexual Intimacy

Ironically, most of the post-1960s parents (and other adults) I work with are even more tongue-tied about sex than generations before. They come to parenting thinking that they are so much more "liberated" than their parents but then cannot understand why they find the subject so daunting to talk about. They know they do not want to give the same messages, spoken or unspoken, they received as children and adolescents, but for the life of them, many cannot figure out what they want to say instead. They know in their gut that the world to which their children have total access has gone upside down concerning sex, yet they have never been taught how to turn it right side up for their kids.

The discourse that has forever been missing from conversations with children and adolescents has been about sex as a profound form of human intimacy. Many parents think that once they have told their children about "sex" (as in, the mechanics of sexual intercourse) and explained that it is supposed to be about "love," they have done the job. Imagine a child trying to piece all that together: The contact between two particular (and according to many children, pretty yucky) body parts means you are in love? Later on, parents may be able to better articulate the connection, but children may have difficulty making sense of it absent an earlier understanding of sexual behavior beyond its mechanics.

If adults hope to make sex as intimacy a real and living concept for their children, they will need to cultivate their own and their children's awareness of the broad concept of human intimacy as an essential—if not quintessential—experience. By underscoring clear examples of physical, social, intellectual, and spiritual intimacy as they are expressed in everyday life, adults can much more readily make gradual and deliberate connections for children between these kinds of experiences and the concept of sex as a form of human intimacy.

For example, rather than talking about "sex" as one particular "act" that joins two particular body parts, adults can describe it as a continuum of intimate touching and physical contact that is sexually arousing—from kissing to various forms of intercourse. Re-conceptualizing sex in this way is also fair and inclusive toward homosexual relationships. After all, defining sex as vaginal intercourse, as is the customary practice, negates the very existence of people who are lesbian, gay, or bi-sexual.

With guidance, young people can more easily understand that just as emotional intimacy involves revealing increasingly personal and private aspects of one's emotional self, sexual experiences involve revealing increasingly personal and private parts of one's physical self. In each case, an increasingly trusting relationship evolves, creating the conditions and context for true intimacy.

Judaism and the Concept of Sexual Intimacy

In the work that I do, I am often dismayed by the fact that many young people do not believe that religion has important things to say about sexuality. Frequently, they identify religious doctrine as "sex-negative"—as teaching only that sex is essentially bad unless it occurs, or is redeemed, under very specific circumstances. Interestingly, I find it is often students from a fundamentalist or evangelical tradition who speak most favorably, and certainly most clearly and authoritatively, about the religious guidance they have received about sex. My Jewish students typically know that sex is considered a mitzvah, but often cannot quite put that together with all of the various sexual prohibitions they know exist in Torah (that is, unless sexuality has been addressed very specifically in their religious education).

Even in secular settings, I like to share my understanding of Jewish teaching about sexuality. I start with the biblical verb for sex—"to know"—as a means to introduce the idea of sex as a form of human intimacy and to make the point that just as emotional intimacy involves deep knowledge of another person, so does sexual intimacy. I often simply ask my students what they think the verb "to know" might mean in relation to sex, and it is amazing how quickly they can begin to think about sex in a deeper, more philosophical context. Indeed, my older students can easily grasp a profound understanding of sex, and other forms of human intimacy, as a means of diminishing the existential aloneness that we all experience as part of human life.

I also like to share how intriguing I find the Creation myth in the Book of Genesis. Once Adam and Eve disobey God and eat from the Tree of Knowledge of Good and Evil, an immediate consequence is the sudden realization of their own nakedness. I think of their covering up as an acknowledgement of the boundaries that exist between us and other people in an imperfect world. In such a world, it becomes safe, as well as a safe haven, to share all of ourselves only within the confines of an intimate, trusting relationship.

By far, my favorite way to talk about Jewish understandings of sex is within the context of *kedushah*, holiness. Just as we keep *Shabbat* holy by keeping it special and uniquely different from all other days of the week, we keep sex holy by treating it with reverence. If we have sex indiscriminately and under ordinary circumstances, it is no longer special and cannot be holy. Also, if I have sex with many people, it means that the person I love is no different from others. If, on the other hand, I reserve sexual intimacy only for one person, not only can the sex itself remain meaningful, but also that person can know that he or she is uniquely meaningful and special to me.

Even my non-Jewish students find this way of conceptualizing sexual intimacy powerful and compelling (not to mention romantic!), quite apart from any particularly religious aspects of the argument. I so appreciate that by using Jewish concepts without preaching, moralizing, or proselytizing, I can make the case easily and convincingly for comprehending sexuality in deeply meaningful ways. I am also acutely aware that how, indeed whether, students apply that understanding in a world where these concepts are rarely if ever reinforced is another matter.

A Revolution in Framing Sexual Values

The 1960s saw unprecedented questioning of authority in all aspects of American life. Centuries-old attitudes about sex suddenly seemed too strict and outdated. Many couples began to ignore the official dictum that sexual intercourse was moral only within marriage, in favor of a contextual and relationship-based ethic. A marriage license is "just a piece of paper," people said. The really important considerations were the quality of the relationship and the degree to which the couple was capable of maturely handling the responsibilities involved.

To many, this change signaled a breakdown in morality, because traditional values such as chastity and monogamy were no longer seen as absolute. What occurred, however, was not so much a breakdown in particular values as a switch to a *different way of framing sexual values*. Sexual morality was no longer defined strictly in categorical terms, in other words, with marital intercourse viewed as automatically "right" and non-marital intercourse as universally "wrong." The morality of a sexual act now depended not on marital status (objectively determined), but on the status of a given relationship (subjectively determined). This was an entirely new way of thinking about sex because that is precisely what was required—thinking.

Whether this shift was fundamentally a good change or not, it nonetheless represented a radical departure from the past and one that we have yet to come to recognize, yet alone come to terms with, as a culture. Truthfully, what the nation experienced in the '60s was not a sexual revolution, but a sexual revolt: We tossed out the old ideas but failed to replace them with anything specific enough to make an ethic out of. Is it surprising, then, that sex is now so frequently depicted as an amoral enterprise—simply another form of entertainment or recreation, deserving no moral reflection of any kind?

Forty years after the revolt, our children are paying the price for all of this ethical sloppiness. With the advent of HIV, we have reduced sexual morality still further to a simple issue of "safety." Ask almost any young person what the phrase "safe sex" means, and he or she will say, "Using condoms." The notions of emotional, social, ethical, or spiritual safety do not even come to mind.

If we want our children to think of sex as a part of the human condition rich with meaning and value, we will have to complete the work of a well-intentioned but long-stalled revolution. If a contextual and relationship-based ethic is what we want our children to adopt (and I hear the majority of parents I work with saying that it is), we will have to figure out how to put real teeth in it by spelling out the specific kinds of moral values—such as honesty, caring, responsibility, privacy, respect, mutual consideration—that we expect young people to bring to any sexual relationship, from first kisses to intercourse in its various forms.

We will also need to explain how and why morality and meaning have something to do with sexual behavior in the first place. Certainly, although most sexual acts do not result in procreation, and many sexual acts do not even have the potential to produce children, human sexuality is nevertheless inherently connected to the awesome powers of creation and regeneration. Sexual acts also have the potential to give great pleasure, to express unparalleled emotional and physical intimacy, and to create great suffering. It can be argued that none of these things should be taken lightly and that all of them have to do with human relations and therefore with morality. Judaism, again, with its emphasis on ethical decision-making and behavior, can provide us a model for making the transition to a contextual system of moral thought.

Protecting Ourselves and Others

The cases presented in this volume highlight clearly the ethical values at stake in couple relationships. They ask us to examine the concept of obligation to self and others whenever there is a sexual connection between two people. At what point in the course of a sexual relationship does the notion of obligation apply? After a kiss? A touch? Only after intercourse? Not at all, if both parties agree? Or, perhaps there is an even more fundamental value at stake. If we feel as human beings that we have an obligation to our friends, neighbors, community, the environment, the homeless, and the poor, why not to someone with whom we have chosen to share our body in an intimate way? Without some level of personal obligation, we are engaging in a form of objectification that itself raises ethical concerns.

58

Sexual behaviors that involve the risk of significant and potentially life-altering physical consequences for self or others raise powerful questions about ethics and obligation. Rachel and Matt's case study underscores the fact that making sexual choices potentially involves not one decision but many: What is my obligation to inform or ask someone about his or her sexual history? How will I know if what I hear is truthful? How well can we negotiate the use of protection against pregnancy and/or disease? What is my obligation to inform—or my right to be informed—if pregnancy or infection occurs?

Sexual decisions entail many of these complex and often subtle dynamics, especially in the social and emotional realms. At first glance, the physical aspects appear to be more concrete and straightforward. After all, almost everyone knows the basic facts: Sexual intercourse can lead to pregnancy and childbearing, both huge responsibilities. A variety of methods of birth control are available to prevent pregnancy until a woman or couple feels ready to take on the obligations of parenthood. Millions of people become infected with an STD every year in the U.S., all with potentially serious health consequences. Quality education and the easy availability of related medical services, including proven prevention strategies, are crucially important in reducing or eliminating these risks.

The ethical issues at stake, whether considered from a moral or religious perspective, are concrete and straightforward as well. Where there is obvious risk to health or life, most everyone would agree that individuals are duty-bound *always and under all circumstances* to protect themselves and others. In the case of an STD, there is always a self and an *other*; in the case of pregnancy there is always a self and potential *others*. Therefore, the ethically correct response to most of the questions posed in this case study seems clear: one must always act on the side of protection.

Teach the Children

So, why, we must ask, are a full 50% of all *adult* pregnancies each year in the U.S. unplanned? Why do we continue to count more than 900,000 teenage pregnancies a year, and millions more cases of sexually transmitted diseases among teens and young adults? Responsible behavior does not occur in a vacuum. America's distant puritanical heritage, kept alive by the continuing and powerful influence of religious fundamentalists on local, state, and federal education and health care policy regarding sexuality and reproduction, have created huge pockets of underserved young

59

people and adults. This abdication by government, and, ultimately, by society, raises ethical questions about the very foundations of our culture.

In conversation with a group of high school girls just this week, I was struck by the toll that our sexually repressed/sexually obsessed culture takes on the ability to think ethically and act responsibility. These 15- and 16-year-olds, many of whom argued strongly for the right to drink and socialize without adults present, and for the benefits of non-relational sexual behavior, nevertheless could not even imagine a conversation with a prospective sexual partner (even a "boyfriend") about previous sexual history. "No way. It's just not going to happen. It *couldn't* happen," they said. In contrast to those in Western Europe—where in many locations comprehensive sexuality education is supported from an early age, and where teens reportedly would consider not taking the proper sexual precautions the moral equivalent of deliberately running a red light—these girls could not bring themselves even to consider doing the "right thing."

My colleagues working at the college level, not surprisingly, tell similar tales. Sexuality education is most effective when it takes place on a continuum of learning from early childhood to early adulthood. It best occurs layer upon layer, as intellectual, social, emotional, and ethical/spiritual developments unfold. Waiting until children are "older" disables them, just as not teaching basic math facts would make learning algebra impossible. When young adults enter college, they inevitably arrive with huge gaps and many misconceptions about sexuality.

Rearing young people in contemporary American society who can make deliberate, sound, humane, and healthy sexual decisions—even on a purely physical level—is a daunting challenge. It requires them to learn to be comfortable with their own bodies and their own sexualities in a culture where many, if not most, adults still have a hard time explaining wet dreams to 11-year olds. It also requires them to learn how to create egalitarian sexual and romantic relationships despite being surrounded by disturbing and dehumanizing gender stereotypes; to forgo the growing sense of entitlement that leads to the perception of sex as a means to personal gratification, rather than to interpersonal discovery; and, within an "anything goes" culture, to acquire a complex blend of information, attitudes, values, and communication skills that can enable responsible and ethical decision making. Thankfully, Judaism has answers—and questions—to guide them successfully through all of these challenges.

Protect and Respect

Jeffrey Burack

A S AN AIDS doctor, every day I see the tragic consequences of failing to communicate about sexual risks. Many of my patients were infected with the human immunodeficiency virus (HIV) before we knew that there was such a thing; many others, infected later, never knew they were at risk. Now trying to live as normal a life as their HIV will permit, they must grapple with questions of what they need to disclose to whom in their intimate relationships. We might ask: Why would anyone with a potentially lethal, sexually transmitted disease (STD) practice anything other than complete honesty and full immediate disclosure?

Because we are human. We are afraid, with good reason, of the stigma and discrimination we might face when people find out. Sometimes we yearn for sexual gratification. We also yearn for intimate relationships, and are afraid to jeopardize those we have or are hoping for. We fear that, especially at the very start of a relationship, negative information about us will make the other flee before giving us a chance. With some justification, we hope that once they get to know us better they may feel it is worth bearing the risk. Many of my patients tell me that if they are upfront about their HIV infection, they may as well not bother trying to date at all. The kindest and most honest among their prospects tell them outright that it simply does not make sense to get close to someone who is HIV-positive.

Many people with HIV are tormented: Do they give up on the possibility of loving relationships altogether? Or do they not reveal their status until someone has come to know and like them, at least a little? Assuming that no sex has happened, at what point does this concealment become unfair, or even a form of entrapment? My patients' responses to this dilemma run the gamut that you might see in any social group. A few, driven by bitterness or shame, adopt a stance that we might call *caveat amator*, "let the lover beware," denying any responsibility to protect their partners. The partners, so the logic goes, ought to assume that they are at risk and protect themselves accordingly. If they do not, too bad for them; the HIV-positive person says, "It is not my problem."

In my experience, such callousness is rare. Mostly, I see good people struggling over what to do. Some warn potential partners that they are HIV-positive; we might call this the "informed consent" stance. Still others go farther, seeking strategies to avoid putting partners at risk at all by limiting their contact to those who are also HIV-positive, or by becoming celibate.

Reason and Lust

For people who do not have HIV, the stakes may seem much lower, but the struggles and the range of moral stances when it comes to prospective sexual partners are the same. Dilemmas arise because sex is not, and never has been, purely procreative. It has multiple consequences and meanings. It may be a way to express feelings for another, or to explore and express one's own physicality, or it may be for sheer pleasure. A sexual act may be mutually sought and lovingly carried out; or it may have much darker purposes, as when rape is used as a weapon of terror. So the sexual experience can range from coerced, through unenthusiastic (to satisfy one's compulsion, one's partner, or some social expectation), to joyous, and to abandoned.

Indeed, the very idea that sex typically results from any kind of decision at all, or always has some purpose, ignores a very important aspect: lust is a powerful and non-rational motivator. This is captured by a Yiddish saying my parents taught me: "*Az der putz shteyt, leygt der seichel in drerd*"—literally, "When the penis stands, the brain lies in the earth." Though I know of no comparable expression of female lust, women too get carried away and take sexual gambles. Without effective contraception, the risk of pregnancy has always made heterosexual intercourse a sort of Russian roulette. Even when pregnancy is not a concern, the risks of disease and emotional injury often loom over these most intimate of human encounters. But we take those risks, for many reasons, or sometimes without reason.

Jewish Sexual Responsibility

Today, when casual partners hook up for sex with no apparent strings attached, it may seem naïve even to talk of obligations to one another. Yet the sorts of questions facing Rachel in the case study still trouble us: What do I have to tell my partner, and does it matter what kind of relationship we have?

Jewish traditions emphasize duties, which in turn rest on timeless ideas about our relationships and responsibilities. I want to focus on two such Jewish principles. First, duties toward *ourselves* flow from the principle that our bodies and lives are the creation and property

62

of the Divine. We do not own our selves, but rather hold and care for them as stewards or custodians. This is why, for example, many Jewish authorities across all denominations forbid smoking cigarettes, since we do not have the right to pollute and to put at grave risk what is not entirely ours. A literal understanding of the source of this duty may suggest a theology that some contemporary Jews do not share. Still, whatever one's beliefs, the idea that we have a duty to care for and protect ourselves that goes beyond just doing what we want may still resonate.

The second Jewish principle I want to highlight is the Golden Rule, first put forward in Leviticus 19:18: "*Ve-ahavta l're'ekha kamokha*," "Love your fellow as yourself." This makes *empathy* an obligation and the chief engine of our duties to others. In our deliberations, we must show respect and consideration for others. We are required to put ourselves in the other's shoes, to think and feel about the impact of our actions.

But how should that impact count in our decision making? And how much? Our specific duties to others derive from the details of our relationships. My obligations toward strangers, neighbors, friends, parents, children, and my spouse may differ in substance and urgency. And in the course of an evolving romantic or sexual relationship, my duties toward the other person also evolve.

How then, should we understand those duties toward lovers and sexual partners? If we take the *Ve-ahavta* seriously, a good starting point might be this: At a minimum, I should treat my partner as I would wish to be treated. I ought, for example, to disclose as much information as I myself would want to have in order to make informed decisions.

But this "informed consent" stance does not go far enough. Taken together, the demands of stewardship and empathy generate additional responsibilities—those of protecting and respecting myself and others. Beyond merely being truthful, I should act to avoid my partner's suffering, even in circumstances in which the partner does not take responsibility for doing so her/himself. If a female partner yearns to go ahead with unprotected sex, it is still the male partner's duty either to insist on contraception, or to limit activity to sexual acts that cannot get her pregnant. If a potential partner insists that she or he does not mind taking the risk, an HIV-positive person likewise still has a duty to insist on using condoms, or to limit their sex to less risky activities.

Pregnancy, STDs, and Other Risks

Let's consider how these duties of protection and respect play out in the issues raised by Rachel and Matt's case. It is a fair assumption that both partners in a casual heterosexual encounter, or even in a serious relationship, want to avoid both pregnancy and STDs. Barrier contraceptive technologies, especially condoms, usually serve both functions, while hormonal contraception prevents pregnancy, but does nothing to prevent STDs.

Each partner has plans and goals; the narratives of their lives are works in progress that could be rudely derailed and irreparably harmed by an unwanted pregnancy. The duties of protection and respect may require that both partners take active steps to prevent unwanted pregnancy, for each member of the couple's own sake and for each other's. Sex carries other risks and complications not eliminated by contraception. Same-sex partners, for example, or any partners having oral sex, run no risk of pregnancy, but may still transmit STDs to one another. These risks can be reduced by choosing safer sexual practices and by using barriers.

But all kinds of sexual interaction may also create complicating expectations, beliefs, or feelings. What one partner intends as a casual encounter may signify to the other an expression of love, or a promise of a more significant, exclusive, or enduring personal relationship. And there may even be duties to others beyond our partners that also bear on how we conduct our sex lives. Sleeping casually with a friend's current or past lover, for example, may jeopardize that friendship and injure the friend.

More remotely, but no less powerfully, in our roles as potential parents, our duties to our future families may include doing our best to stand in a ready, wholehearted, and loving position when that family comes into being. I may violate that duty by recklessly becoming pregnant or impregnating someone else before we are ready for the responsibilities of parenthood. As such, our duties to protect and respect might require the use of effective contraception—even sometimes dual methods if, for example, a woman is using hormonal contraception but STD prevention remains a concern.

In our case, Rachel has reason to suspect that her contraceptives may have failed and wonders whether to take further steps to prevent or terminate a pregnancy. She also wonders whether to tell Matt, and whether to take his wishes into account. Her responsibilities to him certainly *do not* extend either to a duty to terminate a pregnancy, or to a duty to carry a pregnancy to term. This decision, which most directly affects her health and her future, is ultimately hers. Her duties to responsibly safeguard her own body and life take priority.

Based on the empathy argument, however, she also has a duty to inform Matt, especially if she intends to bear a child, and has a duty to consider his wishes. Most of us would care deeply about having our offspring brought into the world, and would want some opportunity for input. Matt's wishes, though, can never be the last word. Matt may believe strongly that abortion is wrong, and he may be prepared for or even enthusiastic about having a child, but these facts cannot force Rachel to carry an unwanted pregnancy. Conversely, Matt's unreadiness for fatherhood cannot compel Rachel to seek an abortion or give her baby up for adoption.

There are even situations in which Rachel's duty to inform Matt would be outweighed by other considerations—if, for example, she has grounds to fear that he'll coerce her one way or the other. And when her choice is to prevent or end a pregnancy, it's not even clear that she always has the duty to inform him. Here, the nature of the relationship comes more substantially into play. A woman coerced into sex is justified in using any means to prevent or end a pregnancy without informing her aggressor. The same may be true when the encounter, though voluntary, was clearly intended by both partners to be casual. The longer and more intimate the relationship, the stronger Rachel's duties are to inform Matt and to consider his wishes. But at no point do Matt's preferences dictate her choice. These standards may seem unfair to male partners who would like to have a say in their reproductive outcomes. But the alternative—limiting women's control over these critical life decisions—is unacceptable. Young men's sexuality education must therefore promote awareness of such potential consequences, since decisions about whether or not to continue a pregnancy may often be out of their hands, and sometimes even hidden from them.

Getting Tested for STDs
Jewish notions of duties to protect and respect demand not only that we take care to avoid STDs, but require other actions of us as well: (1) getting ourselves tested regularly for asymptomatic infections; (2) disclosing risk promptly to partners who may be at risk; and (3) providing comprehensive sexuality education to our youth.

Why do sexually active people not get routinely tested for STDs? Part of the answer is that they may not know they are at risk. Many people do not think that they are at risk for HIV infection, for example, because they do not identify with a known "risk group," such as men who have sex with men or injection drug users. Others have mistaken beliefs about how they might acquire HIV—for example, that if you are the penile insertive partner, you cannot get HIV from vaginal or anal sex. But the reality is that it is not *who you are*, or even primarily *what you do*, but *with whom you do it* that puts you at risk for HIV. If your partner has HIV, you are at risk.

And here is the central problem with HIV as with other STDs: testing and disclosure are essential precisely because infection and transmission can occur when a person has no outward signs or symptoms. There is generally no way to know that a partner has one of these infections unless she or he tells you. What is worse is that the partner may not even know. It is currently estimated that of the approximately 1.1 million Americans infected with HIV, about a quarter do not know they have it. And that quarter, perhaps in part because they do not know they are putting others at risk, transmits more than half of all new HIV infections each year.

Aside from ignorance, there are powerful and complex psychological reasons that people avoid STD testing. These include fear, denial, and the often very real stigma that may accompany even asking for testing, let alone testing positive. Some people who ought to know that they are at high risk for HIV avoid testing because they are afraid to confront the responsibilities that might follow a positive test, including worrying about and taking steps to preserve their own health and disclosing their status to partners. It may feel safer or easier not to know.

One solution to this problem is to make testing universal and routine, thereby removing not only the need for initiative, but also the stigma. Then, being asked to take the test, or agreeing to take it, would no longer be taken to suggest anything about who you are or what you do. Several years ago, the American obstetrics community adopted a standard of routinely testing all pregnant women for HIV, regardless of risk behavior. The results? Women now expect an HIV test as part of the routine panel of pregnancy lab tests, and generally do not object. Women identified as HIV-positive then get effective treatment. As a result, the rate of babies being born with HIV has been cut almost to zero. For these reasons, major health groups like the Centers for Disease Control and Prevention and the American College of Physicians now recommend that all adolescents and adults be routinely offered HIV testing when seeking medical care. Such universal screening must be implemented with the utmost concern for the privacy of those who test positive, the severe discrimination they still face, and the overall impact of a positive result on their lives. Testing without supportive services and referrals is cruel.

The same logic ought to apply to other STDs that are common, often asymptomatic, and transmissible to others—in other words, to all of them. It may not be practical or cost-effective to institute nationwide universal screening for all STDs, but the questions posed by our case are ones of personal morality, not of public policy. It is my duty to get tested for STDs for which I may be at risk, and to consult medical providers for an appropriate testing schedule based on my sexual history and current activity.

Disclosure of Positive STD Results

What, then, ought we do with positive test results? If I discover that I have an STD, it is my duty to think carefully about whom I may have put at risk—typically, anyone with whom I have had sex since my last negative test, or since the episode that could have resulted in my getting infected. It is irrelevant whether partners are those I think may have infected me, rather than those I have potentially exposed; they may not know they are infected, and still need to be informed. It is often difficult to know exactly how far back one's risk realistically goes, and therefore whom one needs to notify. In general, we should consult medical providers or public health personnel to assist in figuring out who may be at risk.

Disclosure to partners, past and current, should be driven by the question of actual risk to them, which at least in part is a function of the curability of the STD. So one need not disclose a past history of syphilis, gonorrhea, or chlamydia to a current partner, assuming that curative treatment was properly completed.

But what about incurable infections like HIV, herpes simplex (HSV), or human papillomavirus (HPV)? Here, things get complicated. Surely, the severity or lethality of the infection would seem to matter. The duty to disclose being HIV-positive would seem more important than the duty to disclose a history of HPV—so are there gradations of duty? And should the medical facts about transmission of different STDs change

67

our assessment of the duties to disclose? Do factors like getting treatment, or using condoms, change the force of our disclosure duties? And what of the many other implications of STDs, such as for bearing and raising children? Pelvic inflammatory disease (PID) caused by gonorrhea or chlamydia is a common cause of female infertility. Surely there is some duty to inform potential life partners about how their expectations of having a family might become complicated. HIV infection complicates reproduction in a variety of ways; but even if safe reproduction can be assured, what of the risk of premature illness or death to an HIV-positive parent? Is the other partner entitled to be warned of these risks in advance?

It may be helpful to consider analogous questions about disclosing one's status as a carrier of Tay-Sachs or other genetic diseases, or, for that matter, details of one's family health history that might confer genetic risk on one's offspring or oneself. What does one have a duty to disclose to a likely life partner? To a potential partner? And when in the course of a relationship are such duties generated?

Finally, are there situations in which other responsibilities might outweigh those of disclosure? How, for example, should one weigh the duty to disclose against the fear of bodily harm from a coercive or intoxicated partner? These difficult questions of personal morality have no simple answers. The duties to protect and respect provide a starting point, from which we may seek clarity in introspection, discussion with confidants, or spiritual counseling.

Practically, the prospect of informing sexual partners of their STD risk is at least embarrassing and painful, and sometimes dangerous. Fortunately, duty may not always require us to tell a current or past partner directly, but rather to make sure that the partner is told. Help is available that can protect one's privacy and dignity, and in some cases allay fears of being disgraced or otherwise harmed by angry partners. Most local, county, or state health jurisdictions provide Partner Counseling and Referral Services (PCRS) that offer two ways to notify potentially at-risk partners. The PCRS programs offer counseling and support for people who choose to notify their partners themselves. For the rest, program personnel will contact partners and inform them that they are at risk, without revealing the identity of the source client. As one might expect, partners often immediately want to know, "From whom did you get this information?" But PCRS programs are required to strictly maintain the confidentiality of the client. Of course in some cases, it is hard to do that—for example, when the partner being notified has had only one sex partner recently, or ever. But trained PCRS personnel discuss these scenarios with clients ahead of time.

The Length of the Relationship as a Factor in Disclosure

What difference does the length of the relationship make in determining a partner's duty to disclose? We are inclined to believe that such duties become stronger as a relationship endures—that the longer we have been with someone, the more truthfulness we owe them. But I want to challenge this view and make the case instead that duty demands early disclosure. Many people are disinclined to disclose their STD status before a first sexual encounter: the risk of transmission from a single encounter may be low, the chance of ruining the occasion high, and there is likely little sense of obligation to the partner. But coming back for a second intimate encounter, whether sexual or not, already says substantially more than the first one did. A second date suggests that something happened on the first worth pursuing; a second time having sex starts to look less like a meaningless hookup. And less so with each further encounter.

Presumably, the partners' commitment to one another grows deeper and more serious with time—partly because they come to know one another more intimately, but also because as time goes by, the very fact of being together makes an increasingly clear statement, publicly and to one another, of their intentions. As the relationship deepens, there is a heightened sense of duty to care for and protect one another and typically a growing sense of trust and safety, as well. So it would seem that with more time together, there should be a stronger obligation to disclose one's sexual history, and especially any STD history that might put the partner at risk.

Paradoxically, though, this kind of disclosure often gets harder and riskier with growing intimacy. The longer you and I have been together, the angrier you might be to find out that I have HIV and did not tell you at the outset, when you would have had the chance to run the other way before becoming involved. Now you have already been exposed. And while you might have understood and forgiven someone who did not disclose her or his status if you were a one-night hook up, you might now ask: What kind of person would hide that information from someone with whom they have been intimate and exclusive for six months?

69

So disclosure often does not happen at a first encounter because the risks—of conflict, humiliation, and loss of the opportunity for intimacy—may not yet be counterbalanced by an intuitive sense of duty to protect the partner. But letting that first chance go by sets a trap, for it only gets harder to disclose as the relationship goes on. This is exacerbated by another dynamic that often sets in regarding the pressure to stop using condoms. Sex partners who start out using barrier methods or otherwise practicing safer sex may decide to "ease up" on infection prevention as they spend more time together and their relationship becomes exclusive. This may well represent a rational evolution in a relationship, especially under the following four conditions: (1) Both partners were tested for STDs at the outset, and again after enough time has elapsed to exclude undiagnosed latent infection. (2) Both partners are monogamous. (3) Contraception is not a concern (e.g., in a same-sex couple, or a heterosexual couple using hormonal contraception). And, importantly, (4) both are explicitly willing to bear the continued risk if it turns out that one of the first three conditions has not been fully met.

Now, let's say one partner, believing these conditions to be met, feels that, for the sake of greater sexual pleasure, it is time to stop using condoms and starts exerting pressure on the other partner to do so. Let's also say that the other partner has not been forthcoming about her or his HIV status. The HIV-positive person is now badly ensnared. She or he may resist the pressure without being able to say why, arousing frustration, indignation, and possibly suspicion on the part of the partner. Or, to avoid conflict, she or he may give in and have unsafe sex. But that would genuinely endanger his or her partner. And if and when the truth does come out, there is far more reason for the partner to be furious. This may all sound like adolescent drama, but it is deadly serious. I know of both women and men who have been killed by long-term partners to whom they eventually revealed their HIV infection.

So both duty and prudence call for disclosure up front, before a relationship is established. This is where duty's demands feel more arduous. Empathy is easy when we are in love; it is natural to want to protect those we are close to. But the *Ve-ahavta* principle insists precisely that we put ourselves in the other's shoes when we would not be emotionally inclined, by familiarity and devotion, to do so. It is especially about the stranger, the first-time partner, that we need to ask: "If our places were switched, would I not want to know if he or she were infected?"

Sex Education

It is also our collective duty to create social conditions under which this sort of disclosure, while never easy, might be made safer and more ordinary. Sexuality education can be one tool for doing this. How best to teach sexual safety, however, remains politically vexed in contemporary America.

But there is, in my view, no place for abstinence-only sex education. This stance is based both on my belief that moralistic curricula can be harmful, and also on empirical observations that abstinence-only education is unrealistic and does not work. In virtually every cultural context, it is clear that people have sex that is not socially sanctioned, be it premarital or extramarital, same-sex or other-sex. Exclusively emphasizing abstinence increases guilt and shame over things that many will end up doing in any case, making them less likely to talk about their concerns or to seek help, and failing to equip them with the skills and knowledge they need to conduct themselves safely. So if youth are going to know about the risks and complications of sexual exploration before it begins, they need systematic education, without assumptions or decrees about what they will or should do and with whom.

Parents, who may be best equipped to transmit values to their children, may choose to promote abstinence for moral or religious reasons. And it is important in any case to convey the real benefits of abstaining from sexual activity until youth are emotionally prepared for both the activity and its consequences, while at the same time enhancing their self-esteem and teaching them skills that will help them resist social and personal pressure to have sex before they are ready. But recognizing that early sex happens, abstinence education should always be offered with an "and if you do..." component that emphasizes how to make sexual relations safer. This combination is referred to as comprehensive sexuality education (CSE).

Study after study demonstrates that comprehensive sexuality education *does not* increase rates of teen sexual activity, but that it *does* reduce rates of teen pregnancy and STDs significantly more than either abstinence-only education or a lack of sex education. Ideally, sexuality education should equip young people to know what they are doing and to take appropriate steps to minimize physical and emotional risks to themselves and their partners. This education should therefore include training in dialogue and negotiation skills with partners, at every age and stage. And it should encourage youth, in developmentally appropriate ways, to think about precisely the issues of protection and respect raised by Rachel and Matt's case. There is little point in knowing about sexual safety, after all, without the moral motivation to seek it or the communication skills to make it happen.

CASE 3

✤

SEX WORK AND PORNOGRAPHY

Case Study

N AOMI IS a 23-year-old female. She has not had a college education and finds herself with several options for supporting herself. She could earn $7.50/hour as a drugstore clerk without benefits, but it is not clear that she could support herself on that wage, and she would likely be fired the first time that she couldn't make a shift because she is too ill to work. Alternatively, she could take a job as a dancer in a strip club, where she could earn significant money for minimal hours' work, and where she would have more flexibility to negotiate her shifts and her hours.

She regards her body as hers to do with as she pleases and regards sex work as, simply, a form of physical labor. At the same time, she recognizes that women's sexuality has been commodified by the broader culture, and is aware that stripping contributes to the objectification of women, generally—and of herself, specifically (even though she is compensated and not bothered by this).

Which job should she take? Why? If she decides to work at the strip club, should she only take the job under certain working conditions? If she had more economic and professional options that would give her the same salary and flexibility, are there reasons that she should not choose this instead? Does the moral status of her accepting this work change if the job were not in a strip club, but rather as a phone sex operator? As a prostitute? If she engaged in any of these activities, would that make her less desirable as a potential mate? Would our understandings of the situation be different in any way if Naomi were a man? Would any of this change if Naomi were working in photography or film, in which a lasting image is created?

Is it morally acceptable to view pornography? Is it permissible to be a patron in a strip club? Is there a difference in how we morally evaluate patrons or consumers of pornography and/or sex work from how we assess those working in the industry? Is there a difference in how we assess workers in the sex industry from how we assess the owners of the establishments in which they work?

Traditional Sources

Compiled by Uzi Weingarten and the Editors

On Licentiousness
1. Maimonides (Rambam), *Mishneh Torah*, Laws of Marriage 1:4

Before the giving of the Torah, a man would meet a woman in the marketplace, and if he and she wanted, he would pay her wages and have sex with her. ... After the Torah was given, the *k'deshah* [prostitute, or possibly cultic prostitute] was forbidden, as it is written: "There shall not be a *k'deshah* among the daughters of Israel" (Deuteronomy 23:18). Therefore whoever has sex with a woman as an act of licentiousness without betrothal has transgressed the prohibition of *k'deshah*.

2. Rabbi Abraham ben David (Ravad) on Maimonides' *Mishneh Torah*, Laws of Marriage 1:4

A *k'deshah* is one who is ready and freely available to all. But one who is exclusive to one man is the concubine (*pilegesh*) mentioned in Scripture, and there is neither a transgression nor a penalty involved.

On Revealing One's Body and Notions of Modesty
3. Babylonian Talmud, *Shabbat* 113b

Rabbi Yohanan called his garments "my honorers."

4. Babylonian Talmud, *Bava Kamma* 86b

Our Rabbis taught: If someone insulted a person who was naked, he would be liable [for paying compensation for *boshet*, the insult and embarrassment involved] though there could be no comparison between one who insulted a person who was naked [in which case the payment would be much less] and one who insulted a person who was dressed. If he insulted him in a public bath, he would be liable [for paying for the insult] though one who insulted a person in a public bath [where the person is already in a state of embarrassment and therefore the penalty would be less] cannot be compared to one who insulted a person in the market place.

The Master said: "If he insulted a person who was naked, he would be liable." But is a person who walks about naked capable of being insulted?—Rav Papa said: The meaning of "naked" is that a wind [suddenly] came and lifted up his clothes, and then someone came along and raised them still higher, thus putting him to shame. "If he insulted him in a public bath, he would be liable." But is a public bath a place where people are apt to feel offended [by means of being uncovered, since everybody is uncovered there]?—Rav Papa said: It means that he insulted him [by uncovering him] near the river [where people merely bathe their legs and are otherwise fully dressed].

5. Mishnah, *Sanhedrin* 6:3

When they brought [a person condemned to death] within four cubits of the place of stoning, they would strip the person of his or her clothes. They would cover a man [in the genital area] in front; a woman they would cover in the front and back, according to Rabbi Yehudah. But the Sages say: A man is stoned naked, but a woman is not stoned naked.

6. Joseph Caro (16th century, Spain and Israel), *Shulchan Arukh, Orach Chayyim* 240:6, 11 (with glosses by Rabbi Moses Isserles, 16th century, Poland)

6. It is forbidden for a man to engage in sexual relations in front of anyone who is awake, even if there is a partition of ten cubits [fifteen feet] height between them, but in front of a baby who does not know how to speak it is permitted….

11. It is forbidden to engage in sexual relations in the light of a candle, even if he covers it with his *tallit*. *Gloss: But if he makes a partition of ten cubits in front of the candle, even if the light can be seen through the partition—as, for example, he interposed a sheet— that is permissible….* And it is also prohibited to engage in sexual relations during the daytime unless it is in a darkened house. *Gloss: He may darken it with his tallit, and then relations are permissible.*

On Treatment of Employees
7. Leviticus 19:13

You shall not defraud your fellow. You shall not commit robbery. The wages of a laborer shall not remain with you until morning.

8. Deuteronomy 24:14–15

You shall not abuse a needy and destitute laborer, whether a fellow countryman or a stranger in one of the communities of your land.

You must pay him his wages on the same day, before the sun sets, for he is needy and urgently depends on it; else he will cry to the LORD against you, and you will incur guilt.

9. Mishnah, *Bava Metzi'a* 7:1

If one hired workers and instructs them to begin work early and to stay late, in a place in which it is not the custom to begin work early and to stay late, the employer may not force them to do so. In a place in which it is the custom to feed the workers, he must do so. In a place in which it is the custom to distribute sweets, he must do so. Everything goes according to the custom of the locale.

A story about Rabbi Yohanan ben Matya: He told his son, "Go, hire us workers." His son went and promised them food [without specifying what kind or how much]. When he returned, his father said to him, "My son! Even if you gave them a feast like that of King Solomon, you would not have fulfilled your obligation toward them, for they are the children of Abraham, Isaac, and Jacob. However, as they have not yet begun to work, go back and say to them that their employment is conditional on their not demanding more than bread and vegetables." Rabbi Shimon ben Gamliel said, "It is not necessary to make such a stipulation. Everything goes according to the custom of the locale."

10. Babylonian Talmud, *Bava Metzi'a* 83a

We need [this statement that specifies that an employer may not force workers to begin early and stay late] for the case in which the employer raises the workers' wages. In the case in which he says to them, "I raised your wages in order that you would begin early and stay late," they may reply, "You raised our wages in order that we would do better work."

Contemporary Sources

Compiled by Steven Edelman-Blank

1. Leah Furman, *Single Jewish Female: A Modern Guide to Sex and Dating* (New York: Perigee, 2004), 115

Whether we dress provocatively to engage male attention or simply to show off the fruits of our labor at the gym, the results are often the same: Our focus shifts away from hearts and minds and onto our bodies. The flaunt-it-if-you've-got-it attitude so encouraged in our society runs counter to Judaic values, which stress inner beauty and self-confidence over the arrogance and self-conceit that are the inevitable results of concentrating too much on appearances.

2. Diablo Cody, *Candy Girl: A Year in the Life of an Unlikely Stripper* (New York: Gotham Books, 2006), 25

You know how in the lyrics to "Tangled Up in Blue" Dylan mentions going to a topless bar and staring at a girl's face? He lied. Nobody looks at your face when you're naked—not even nice Jewish boys like Zimmy.

Note: Bob Dylan's real name is Robert Zimmerman.

3. Sarah Katherine Lewis, *Indecent: How I Make It and Fake It as a Girl for Hire* (Emeryville, CA: Seal Press, 2006), 319, 321

The truth is that I love the industry for what it's given me. I've spent ten years moving my body for a living, on my own terms. When I think about all the other jobs a young woman can get with no work experience and no education—food service, office work, retail—I know that if I were doing it all over again I'd pick the sex industry over those options every single time, even knowing exactly how ugly and soul-killing it can get. The truth is I'm not good at working for other people, and I'm sure as hell not good at being told what to do. It also turns out I'm a hard worker—I just need a huge amount of personal autonomy. With it, I can roll in filth and still feel better about myself than I ever felt wiping down tables or making coffee…

But my main problem with the adult industry is simply this: When we take part in it, we increase our alienation from each other. We become objects to each other, whether we're cash-vending objects or pleasure-vending objects. We take something as beautiful and communicative as sexual ecstasy and we commodify it, and in doing so we destroy everything that it stands for. We're not making love. As sex workers we're performing acts that we'd rather not be performing, with people we don't care about, because it is better than starving or working in a labor system that doesn't meet our needs. Or if we're customers, we're buying a poor semblance of affection that's so transparently false it bears almost no similarity to anything done in the spirit of honest love—and we know it, but we still seek out that kind of sexual service because it's easier or less frightening than trying to obtain the real thing.

4. **Nina Hartley, "Confessions of a Feminist Porno Star" in *Sex Work: Writings by Women in the Sex Industry*, 2nd edition, Frédérique Delacoste and Priscilla Alexander, eds. (San Francisco, CA: Cleis Press, 1998), 142**

I find performing in sexually explicit material satisfying on a number of levels. First, it provides a physically and psychically safe environment for me to live out my exhibitionist fantasies. Secondly, it provides a surprisingly flexible and supportive arena for me to grow in as a *performer*, both sexually and non-sexually. Thirdly, it provides me with erotic material that I like to watch for my own pleasure. Finally, the medium allows me to explore the theme of celebrating a positive female sexuality—a sexuality that has heretofore been denied to us. In choosing my roles and characterizations carefully, I strive to show, always, women who thoroughly enjoy sex and are forceful, self-satisfying and guilt-free without also being neurotic, unhappy, or somehow unfulfilled.

5. **Tamar Fox, "Porn: Trying To Make It Look Good (And Failing)," *Jewcy*, posted June 5, 2007. Available at http://www.jewcy.com/ faithhacker/porn_trying_to_make_it_look_good_and_failing**

There is simply no justification for pornography in any facet of the Jewishly engaged world. No one is saying it's okay. Of course, that hasn't kept Jews out of the business. Ron Jeremy and Nina Hartley are Jewish, and here at Jewcy we've brought you interviews with Jewish porn star and producer Joanna Angel, as well as an interview with her distraught Jewish mother. You can even find an academic article on Jews in the porn industry over at the Jewish Quarterly. But no matter how hard I looked, I couldn't find any publication, organization or blog willing to rave about how Jews in porn is a good or even acceptable thing.

When I finished reading through all of these discussions and articles it occurred to me that what I'd been looking for was something that would let my friend off the hook. I wanted some rabbi somewhere to be giving away free heters [permissive rulings] to porn stars. But there doesn't appear to be any such rabbi. And the more I think of that, the more I'm okay with it, even proud of it. I've written before about how important I think it is for us to provide realistic sex education and information to the frum [religious] community, but I'm relieved to find that even I have clear boundaries. And pornography is way out of bounds.

6. Andrea Dworkin, "Against the Male Flood: Censorship, Pornography, and Equality" in *Letters From A War Zone: Writings 1976–1987* (London: Secker and Warburg, 1988), 264

In the amendment to the Human Rights Ordinance of the City of Minneapolis written by Catherine A. MacKinnon and myself, pornography is defined as the graphic, sexually explicit subordination of women, whether in pictures or in words, that also includes one or more of the following: women are presented dehumanized, as sexual objects, things, or commodities; or women are presented as sexual objects who enjoy pain or humiliation; or women are presented as sexual objects who experience sexual pleasure in being raped; or women are represented as sexual objects tied up or cut up or mutilated or bruised or physically hurt; or women are presented in postures of sexual submission; or women's body parts are exhibited, such that women are reduced to those parts; or women are presented being penetrated by objects or animals; or women are presented in scenarios of degradation, injury, abasement, torture, shown as filthy or inferior, bleeding, bruised or hurt in a context that makes these conditions sexual.

7. Shmuley Boteach, *Kosher Sex: A Recipe for Passion and Intimacy* (New York: Doubleday, 1999), 114–115

Judaism, as one might expect, tends to oppose pornography. This is not because Judaism toes the prudish line of the religious "right," opposing pornography purely because it is indecent and immoral. Nor does it take the "leftist" position that argues that it denigrates human sexuality and primarily degrades women. Although all these things may be true about pornography, they are not the root of the problem.

The issue for Judaism is that pornography does not enhance the passion and romance between a couple, but, rather, replaces them by something alien. As the purpose of sex is to foster and sustain emotional intimacy between husband and wife, whatever a couple does is permitted if it leaves their passion for each other intact. Here lies the problem, for in most cases pornography will serve as an end in itself rather than as a tool for the excitement of passion.

Responses

The Realities and Ethics of Sex Work: An Interview with Ron Jeremy

Elliot N. Dorff

The following is a transcript of an interview that Elliot Dorff conducted with Ron Jeremy in Los Angeles on August 13, 2008.

Elliot Dorff: Ron, in the case about Naomi, what do you think she should do?

Ron Jeremy: Whether or not to engage in sex work is a person's own moral choice. The decision should depend on what the individual feels about it. I would not tell this girl what to do; I have no right. But, of course, as I am in the adult industry, I do not find anything wrong with it. I believe that even from a religious point of view, adults choosing to do sexual things for consenting adults to watch is okay with the Lord above, as long as nobody is being forced, coerced, pushed or whatever else. I think pornography has a right to exist....

Very fine lines distinguish the various forms of adult entertainment, including dancing topless, doing magazine work alone (like maybe *Hustler*, *Penthouse*, *Playboy*), doing magazine work with another guy or girl, and ultimately, hardcore movies. It's all a matter of where you draw the line.

We all draw our own lines. Even in the religious world, this happens. My brother worked in the Catskill Mountains, as did I. He worked at a very religious place called the Tanzville Hotel. A lot of the religious Jews would not operate machinery on the Sabbath. But yet if he, or a Christian person, turned on a TV set, they could then watch TV. They could ride in a car if someone else was driving it, because *they* cannot operate machinery, but others may. But it is basically the same thing if you are enjoying what is on TV, no matter who turned it on. We are all hypocrites in a way.

ED: Do you really think that all moral lines are hypocritical? Or that people who assert moral distinctions are all hypocrites?

RJ: No, not every person or every line. It is just that so many people who judge others morally do not abide by the very standards they use to criticize others. Still, although some lines we draw are hypocritical, some are not.

I think that it is correct that Naomi may choose what she does with her own body. She has to accept the fact that there is a double standard in society. The double standard was not created by the porn business; it is there because of her upbringing.

We raise our children unevenly. It is not fair, but it exists. All over the world we tell our boys, "Go get 'em son, make Dad proud." "Hey honey, look at all the girls chasing junior! He's gonna grow up to be one stud muffin." In contrast, to our daughters we say, "Don't you dare! You wait to have sex until you're married, wait until there are feelings of love and mutual commitment. Don't you be a whore!" You do not picture a father saying to his wife, "Hey honey, look at all the boys chasing Mary." In fact, if that were true, the father might say, "Get the gun!" We have a wholly different attitude toward our sons and daughters. We raise them with uneven upbringings that are causing these problems for Naomi now.

When it comes to pay, there is a double standard in the reverse direction. I voted for the Equal Rights Amendment, so did all my friends, so did most of the porn business. But, as Susan Cole[1] has pointed out, in the adult industry, girls make way more money than guys. I work for women, women run most of the adult companies: Jenna Jameson, Candida Royalle, Tera Patrick, Jesse Jane, and on and on. They have their own websites, their own businesses, their own corporations: Danni Ashe, Asia Carrera, and so on. These girls are becoming multimillionaires, and they boss around the men.

In the name of equality are you going to get someone like Jenna Jameson to give back the $14 million that she made on the sale of Club Jenna to Playboy? Should she give back that money and go back to McDonalds? Hell, no! She is a multimillionaire, and she is going to enjoy it.

The point is, it is unfair that in the adult industry girls make more than men. And it is unfair that if a female porn star or executive became a secretary or did some other job for which she might be qualified, the likelihood is that she would earn very little and maybe not get medical and other benefits. It is unfair that it is like that. Women should get equal pay for equal work. But so should men.

---

1. Susan Cole is an author, playwright, and activist involved in the anti-porn movement.

I was raised by a feminist. If you read my autobiography, which is a *New York Times* bestseller, you would know that my Mom was a lieutenant, a decoder, and a spy during World War II. She worked for the OSS, which later became the Central Intelligence Agency. After the war, to balance work with raising me, she would share jobs at *The New York Times*, where she worked as an indexer, and later for Paramount, where she was in public relations. She had responsible, well-paying jobs back in those days. She also was a college graduate; she graduated from Queens College, where I went to school as well. So my mother was one of the original feminists back in the '40s. As a result, I understand women who work, who want to make equal pay for equal work, and I always supported that. So it is not our fault that the adult industry is one of the few places where women can make way more money than the men make.

ED: How much of a discrepancy in pay is there?

RJ: A girl acting as a porn star can make up to $3,000 a scene, even up to $10,000 a scene if she is under contract. The man who has sex with her makes $300 a scene. So she is making ten times what he makes. Why is that? Because in a heterosexual porn film, the girl is the one who is the fantasy that will sell the film, not the guy. (In gay porn, men make the big bucks, of course, but then they are the fantasy.)

There is another kind of double standard. Men will give male porn stars the thumbs up, telling them that they want to be like them. Behind their backs, they will still say that. People shower female pornographic stars with all kinds of accolades in public, but behind their backs some people call them sluts.

I do not want to exaggerate this, though. Women in the adult entertainment industry do not come across nasty name-calling all that much any more. I have been to a lot of trade shows, and you can watch the Adult Awards on Showtime. You see these women getting awards for best actress, best supporting actress, and so on. You have regular films like *Caligula*, which is hardcore but has mainstream stars in it. Or take, as another example, *The Brown Bunny*. In that movie, Chloe Sevigny, who was nominated for an Academy Award for *Boys Don't Cry* and who acted in *Big Love* on HBO, did a hardcore oral scene with Vincent Gallo, who produced and directed *Buffalo 66* (also an A-list actor). So as the industry achieves more, it makes it easier for girls to explain to their parents that what they are doing is a performance for the camera, just as Chloe Sevigny does.

ED: Do you have any concerns for the health and safety of those in the adult entertainment business? I am thinking of sexually transmitted diseases and, in the case of prostitutes, the risk of assault and even murder. What precautions should Naomi take if she wants to get into this business?

RJ: If Naomi chooses to do dancing, or to be an escort, she should do it carefully, she should do it properly, she should not do it as a streetwalker, she should do it for, let's say, someone who takes care of his or her girls, like Heidi Fleiss, Executive Madam.[2] Whatever she chooses to do, she should try to be good at it—indeed, the best—just as you would strive to be in any other profession. I am not endorsing prostitution, but I am saying that if you choose to do that, you must do it right. You go to the BunnyRanch in Nevada, where it is legal and regulated in both the health and business aspects of the profession. You then bank your money because you will not be able to do this forever.

In general, prostitution is very different from working in adult pornographic films. On the one hand, there is less control over the men involved, who may be infected with a sexually transmitted disease or treat the woman badly. On the other hand, some point out that prostitution is better than acting in adult pornographic films because the woman will not be seen on camera. When she gets married years later and has children and goes to the PTA meeting, no one is going to say, "Aren't you Debbie from *Debbie Does Dallas*?" So there are advantages and disadvantages to both.

Health is, of course, a major concern, and it is totally under control in Nevada, where prostitution is both legal and regulated. I would definitely not suggest that Naomi should work on Sunset Boulevard as a street hooker. If she did, she would go to jail and probably be attacked, raped, diseased, or what have you. If she does it properly, at a bunny ranch where it is legal, it is a whole different thing. Doing legal escort at a government-sanctioned, -controlled, and -licensed brothel is a far cry from being a street hooker on Sunset Boulevard! If a girl wants to be a street hooker, my sympathy goes out to her. That is just a walking disaster area.

---

2. Heidi Fleiss, known as "The Hollywood Madam," was sentenced in 1997 for pandering and tax evasion related to her prostitution ring.

ED: Aside from the health and safety aspects of adult entertainment, how do you understand the moral status of adult entertainment in its various expressions—pornographic films, prostitution, topless dancing, sexually arousing phone conversations, and so on?

RJ: It boils down to moral choices. Keep in mind that one person's morality is not somebody else's. Those who have a religious upbringing and think that doing this kind of work is beneath them *should not do it*! The case as presented suggests that Naomi has only two choices, but I do not believe that Naomi's only alternative is to work in a drugstore that does not give her medical benefits.

For God's sake, honey, go back to school and learn some kind of trade! This is America! You can get another job! Naomi does not have to go from a drugstore to topless dancing. If she has only those two choices, she is seriously brain dead. Under those circumstances, maybe she should be a topless dancer and not think twice.

Naomi should know, though, that porn is very tough. Escorting is very tough. Even topless dancing is very tough. The work itself is hard, and in addition, you have to tolerate the fact that people are going to look down on you for this. But it is not your fault that they are! To most men it is the old story: as long as their mom or sister or daughter does not do it, they will look at someone else's daughter dancing. This is a fact of life. It is the way most people think of the adult entertainment business; it is their moral choice. But Naomi also has the right to make her own moral choices, and so if she wants to do it, she certainly should do it ….

If Naomi chooses to dance, she must accept the fact that others will look down on her. The same is true if she chooses to act in pornographic movies. She will have many fans. People will be showering her with accolades all over the world. If she is halfway good at this, she will be flown to different video stores for appearances all over the world, and she will make lots of money. But yes, some will call her a slut behind her back. If they call her that to her face, she needs to have a boyfriend, a roadie, or a manager who will punch them in the head for it. I cannot imagine someone calling Jenna Jameson a name like that, because thanks to porn she's very rich….

If Naomi does decide to work in our industry, she needs to know that people are going to call her names behind her back. But they are wrong.

And if she can handle it, she can look them back in the eye and say, "Hey, you're watching my films!" or "Hey, I'm not a dope, I choose to do this." If she can walk away with a good sense of herself and her values, then she should go for it.

ED: Even granting that people will evaluate the morality of various actions and professions differently, would you make any distinctions among the various forms of adult entertainment?

RJ: As I said earlier, I would certainly distinguish legal activities from illegal ones, and forms of adult entertainment that include protections for health and safety over those that do not. Other than that, though, I think that it should be a person's own choice as to whether to earn money this way or not—and, for that matter, to use the services of adult entertainment or not.

It is really stupid, though, to equate adult porn with kiddie porn [that is, pornography involving children] or sex with animals! I have never seen either of those in my 30 years in the business. We do not break the law, thank you. So people who want to lump all of adult entertainment into one big category of perversity are ignoring tremendous, important differences between what is legal and what is not, and between what is moral and what is not.

ED: What are some of the ways in which the industry seeks to protect its own?

RJ: There are plenty of girls working in adult entertainment who are perfectly happy and healthy doing it. In part, that is because we have organizations and standards in porn that look to the health and safety of our workers. One is called AIM (Adult Industry Medical Health Care Foundation), which is run by Dr. Sharon Mitchell. Also, porn stars must continually be tested for HIV.

We also have an organization called PAW (Protecting Adult Welfare), which counsels girls who want to get into the business about their choices. They point out that a girl can decide whether she is willing to be photographed in various positions, whether she will do anal sex before the camera, whether she will work with guys only, girls only, both or neither. And if they feel a girl is getting into the business for the wrong reasons, they will do their best to get her out of it. So we try to look after our own.

We take these steps in part because we want to protect those who work in the industry, but another reason is because if we did not do this, the government would breathe down our necks. As Paul Cambria,[3] a lawyer in the adult industry, said, if we do not deal with our own dirty laundry, they will do it for us. They will impose rules and sanctions that will make our heads spin. So we get permits from the appropriate government departments for the sites where we shoot the films. This includes the Fire Marshal and the Board of Health. The Board of Health also looks at how we monitor our blood tests, and so far they have approved how we do it and have not intervened. Cal/OSHA (California Occupational Safety and Health Administration) looks at the working conditions of our workers to make sure that they fulfill state requirements.

ED: Would you distinguish between the morality of people who work in the industry and those who are its patrons and consumers?

RJ: Legally speaking, except in controlled places like bunny ranches in Nevada, both a prostitute and her male client have broken the law. In contrast, adult pornography is 100% legal. So more than distinguishing between actors and consumers, we need to distinguish between various elements of the adult entertainment industry. Escorting is legal in some places, not in others, while adult pornography is legal everywhere as long as it is not foisted on children or on anyone who does not want to see it.

It is interesting to me that sometimes the guy takes an even bigger beating for engaging in prostitution than the girls take. New York Governor Eliot Spitzer, who got caught with his pants down, had to resign from office, his marriage has been in trouble, and he got slammed in the media because as a prosecutor he sent prostitutes to jail. It is the hypocrisy that people do not forget. The lady, though, now goes on to try to make movies, get famous, do commercials. President Clinton was impeached for his affair, and Monica Lewinsky became an instant media star.

If just a regular Joe had an escort, though, we usually think of the escort as being more immoral. This is really wrong because it takes one to have the other. If there were no "Joe" in the world, there would be no escorting in the world either. I look at them as being equal, but I

---

3. Paul Cambria is a lawyer for the adult industry most famous for representing Larry Flynt, publisher of *Hustler* magazine.

think at lot of the public thinks that she is the loose one, she is the more "immoral" one.

The owner of the establishment in which adult pornography is filmed is often seen as simply a business person, but this is all wrong. He or she is just as involved as the actors and producers are. Owners are in the same category, but they can go to their church or temple and tell all their friends that they own a furniture store. People on camera cannot do that. So owners can hide what they are doing better, along with the cameraman, director, assistant director, and so on, but they are all just as morally responsible for the finished product as the actors are.

The owners, though, are generally not hiding any more. The biggest names in the business are out there fighting the fight for First Amendment rights; they belong to the Free Speech Coalition.[4] They go on camera. Steve Hirsch,[5] Marc Cherry, and the women who own companies are all very vocal. They do not hide. In the '70s and the '80s, the owners would hide behind their business, where they would use fake names for themselves and their company, their supposedly legitimate business. Now they are pretty much out there. Their businesses are more accepted now, for pornography is on cable, satellite, the Internet, and DVD. You see it in your own home; it is not primarily seen in theaters that show X-rated movies in scrungy areas of town. That makes it more of a private thing and therefore less threatening to those who do not want to see pornography or allow for public showing of it in theaters.

ED: In what ways, if any, do your Jewish identity and background influence your choice of career and your views of pornography?

RJ: I find that Jews by nature seem to be fairly liberal. Jews do not adhere to the notion that people who work in pornography have been taken over by the devil, that they are "going to burn in hell." I am a good Jewish boy; I celebrated my bar mitzvah at age 13, as did my brother. My sister celebrated her bat mitzvah. I am proud of my religion. I have not been very religious, I have not gone to temple a lot as I should, but I

---

4. The Free Speech Coalition is a trade association for the adult entertainment industry that focuses on combating censorship and defending freedom of expression.
5. Steve Hirsch is President and co-founder of Vivid Video.

respect my religion and I am proud to be a part of it. You will not find a big problem with sex in the Jewish religion, as you will in others.

Along those lines, it is interesting to note that there are many Jewish men in the business, but very few Jewish women. I think the reason for that is that Jewish women are encouraged to go to college, and most women who go to college do not choose to be part of adult movies. The majority of girls in porn are not college educated. If you are going to go to school all these years, you might as well use your brains and your career. There is nothing wrong with porn, but it usually involves only those women who have not had a higher education.

Also, Jewish women know their dads would kill them if they found out what they were doing to earn a living. It is not an easy thing for Jewish parents to understand, and I respect that. I personally see nothing wrong with pornography, but it is hard to convince parents that it is okay for their daughter to be doing this. There is a very strong bond in Jewish families, especially between a father and daughter, and I feel that a girl fears that she would break her father's heart.

As a result, there are very few Jewish women in the industry. Nina Hartley, Heather Hart, Robyn Burke, Laura Leonard, Alexandra Silk— at the moment those are the only Jewish women I can think of in the business.

The same reasoning does not apply to Jewish men, who in large numbers are involved in both acting and production, and who usually have college degrees. Maybe ten times as many Jewish men are involved in the industry as Jewish women. This is the double standard again. It is wrong to have that double standard, but it exists, as these numbers demonstrate.

ED: The Jewish tradition does have a positive attitude toward sex, as you said, but it prizes sex within marriage. Do you think that acting in or watching pornographic films has an effect on marriage? If so, what do you think it is?

RJ: I have always heard the old adage that an escort makes the best wife. I think porn stars make great wives and husbands because they have had their thrill. They do not need to have that kink anymore. They do not need to have wild days of one-night stands because they have had them already. As a result, when these people settle down, they often are married for life. They are not going to get excited by another piece of flesh. Been there, done that!

The Sex of Work, The Work of Sex
Hanne Blank

N AOMI, the young woman in the case study's hypothetical scenario, is not really so hypothetical. Many women are faced with the decision of whether to enter into sex work. Some, including myself and others I have known and cared about, have decided that at one time or other, for some reason or another, sex work was a viable option. In my perspective—which is not just that of a sometime sex worker, but also that of a writer, historian, and educator on sexuality and women's issues—I believe there are numerous reasons that sex work may be an appropriate and indeed ethical, although probably not ideal nor unproblematic, choice of employment.

The Role of Sex in Women's Work

In considering any question about sex work, it is important to note that much of all work available to women is in some respect sex, or at least sexualized, work. Women are constantly evaluated and rewarded in the workplace according to their appearance and their sexual appeal. Even leaving aside the question of the metaphorical "casting couch," or other overtly sexual situations women may be put in by employers, silent prejudice based on appearance remains a real and significant phenomenon.

Repeated studies have proven that in job interviews, for example, the more conventionally pretty and attractive a woman is, the more likely she is to get hired and to get paid more.[1] Indeed, when hiring employees who will interact with the public, employers will often go out of their way to find good-looking people. For instance, attractive appearance and an alluring voice are genuine job skills for many receptionists, flight attendants, and industry conference booth workers (often called "booth bunnies," a reference to the *Playboy* Bunny), to name just a few.

Such privileging of physical appeal is but the tip of the iceberg. In the workplace, many women regularly have to deal with sexual teasing and harassment from other workers. Women working in jobs where they

---

1. See, for example, Senior, Thompson, et al., "Interviewing Strategies in the Face of Beauty: A Psychophysiological Investigation into the Job Negotiation Process," *Annals of the New York Academy of Sciences* v. 1118 (28 Nov 2007), 142–62.

deal with the public, such as the drugstore job that is one of Naomi's choices in this case study, also often find that they are expected to take sexual comments and come-ons from customers in stride. If they do not, customers may complain, and workers can be punished or even lose their jobs for "poor customer service." In some lines of work, the expectation of sexualized interaction with customers is an unwritten, yet explicit, part of the employment. For instance, in most parts of the U.S., restaurant table staff are not even paid minimum wage; they are expected to make most of their income from tips. Waitresses learn quickly that flirting with customers is part of earning enough money to survive.

Many working women, in other words, perform sexual labor of various kinds for pay on a regular basis, even though they do not technically work in the sex industry. It's been argued that even stay-at-home married motherhood, historically touted as the most virtuous of female occupations, is a form of sex work since it is the exchange of sexual access, reproduction, and the "women's work" of childrearing and domestic labor for the financial support of a man.

It would be both untrue and unhelpful, then, to suggest that Naomi has any available employment prospect here that would keep her from being sexually objectified or from having to engage in some form of sexualized work. The question is not whether Naomi is going to have at least some aspect of her livelihood depend on the fact that she may, in a variety of ways, be considered a sexual object. By virtue of being a woman living in a sexist and heterosexist society, she inevitably will. The questions are whether she will be an active or a passive participant in this process, whether it will hurt her or help her, and whether or not she will be allowed autonomy in making sexual decisions.

Views of Women in Jewish and Mainstream Culture

As a feminist, a historian, and a Jew, I feel the obligation, in the interest of social justice, to look carefully at all these issues and more when attempting to answer questions like these. I know from my intellectual and historical work that, in general, patriarchies (I use the word here in the anthropological sense to denote cultures whose order [Greek *arche*] is ruled by males [Greek *patri*]) have tended to limit women's sexual behavior in the interest of easing tensions among men about sex, property, and inheritance. This pattern clearly holds true within both traditional and much of contemporary Judaism.

It is historically, as well as currently, true that notions of female sexual "virtue" in Judaism, or in any cultural group, often depend primarily on whether women conform to these patriarchal priorities. Not surprisingly, women who act with sexual autonomy have traditionally been vilified, although the degree to which this is true has changed over time. We see it in Torah: Deuteronomy 22 authorizes death by stoning of any woman "proven" to have falsely presented herself as a virgin at marriage,[2] and the virtuous Tamar in Genesis 38 is initially attacked for her "whoredom" until she manages to prove that her actions were purposeful and just. We still see it in stereotypes of "Nice Jewish Girls" who do not have sex before marriage (and even then only do it because their husbands want them to), and in depictions of "Jewish American Princesses" who use sex to manipulate men into giving up money and gifts.[3]

The deep-seated suspicion of how women use their sexual agency presents itself in numerous ways. We see it reflected in traditional rules and customs, many of which are not exclusively Jewish, that prohibit women and girls from doing things that might be construed as sexually charged self-presentation: singing or dancing in front of men, for instance, or sporting uncovered hair or legs. We see it in mainstream culture in stereotypes that get applied to sexually assertive women (e.g., that they are sluts, nymphomaniacs, or gold diggers), and those that get applied to sex workers (e.g. that they are sexually indiscriminate or habitual criminals).

Were sexual autonomy for women not so universally suspect, we might not be analyzing this case at all. Consider for a moment that we are not thinking about whether Naomi should take a job as a swimsuit model or as a Vegas showgirl. These jobs are more or less the equal of stripping in terms of job skills, physical exposure, and sexual objectification and exploitation, but because the context is not so explicitly sexual we think of them in an entirely different light.

The fight against sexism, misogyny, and the refusal to grant sexual autonomy has for many years been part of my understanding of what is required for *tikkun*, or repair of the world we live in. The patriarchal

---

2. See my *Virgin: The Untouched History* (New York: Bloomsbury, 2007) for more on this, specifically Chapter Six, "The Blank Page."
3. Beck, Evelyn Torton. "From 'Kike' to 'Jap': How Misogyny, Anti-Semitism, and Racism Construct the Jewish American Princess" in *Race, Class, and Gender*, Margaret Andersen and Patricia Hill Collins, eds. (Belmont, CA: Wadsworth, 1992), 87–95.

attitude toward the "appropriate" relationship between biological sex (maleness/femaleness) and sexuality, which simultaneously insists that women accept the chore of tending to men's sexual desires and demonizes women's autonomous sexuality, represents one of the most fundamental manifestations of social injustice in human cultures. It is old, pervasive, and very slow to change.

Class, Wealth, Education, Capitalism

These issues of sex, sexuality, misogyny, and gender are not the only social justice concerns present in this case study. Issues of class, wealth, education, and capitalism are all evident in the information we have about Naomi, too.

Although we are not told Naomi's socioeconomic background, we do know that she has no college education, which in contemporary America means that she is probably not considered middle-class. The jobs that are open to her are likewise not jobs that will be considered middle-class or jobs that can support a middle-class standard of living. And both jobs subject employees to negative stereotypes; for instance, that people who work lower-class jobs are of limited intelligence, uncaring, or simply cannot do better. Such class prejudice can make it difficult or impossible for the working class to get access to education or training, to say nothing of better jobs.

Another issue here is the function of the working classes in capitalism. Workers under capitalism are exploited for the benefit of corporations and their owners. Working-class labor, which includes the sex industry, depends on a large pool of mostly young, lower-class, less-educated workers who essentially do not have the option of refusing to work whatever jobs are available. The worker pool is larger than the number of available jobs, so workers are considered replaceable. Thus, it is not important to employers to offer workers any safer or better working conditions than the law demands, let alone benefits like health care or paid sick leave.[4] Employers often squash attempts to unionize for better working conditions and pay. Workers see disproportionately little of the profits their work helps to produce. Yet they must survive, and so they cannot afford to quit.

---

4. The absence or erosion of laws requiring employers to provide such benefits, in the U.S. particularly, is another part of the problem, and can be seen as evidence of governmental support of capitalist exploitation.

Sex work, because of its marginal and sometimes illegal status, tends to pay better than most other working-class jobs. This is where sex work—although still a capitalist industry, make no mistake—has its biggest advantages. Sex work is famously easy to get and has little to do with skills or education. The hours are often very flexible. While there is some risk of physical or sexual violence in many kinds of sex work, this is not always the case (phone sex, for example, is very low risk), and in any event, many jobs not classified as sex work are equally or more risky. Sex work is also famously short term; workers often do not stay at the same job for long before moving on, and this is considered normal.

All in all, many women find that despite its drawbacks, sex work can be a better bargain for their time, energy, and labor than "nonsexual" jobs. It was that for me during the period when I was young and had few job skills but needed a job that paid enough to live on while also allowing me to accept career-building, arts-related engagements that paid little or nothing. Furthermore, like many other women I have known who have worked in the sex industry, I found the frankness of sex work a relief. Knowing up front that your work is going to consist of dealing with someone else's sexual desires can be vastly preferable to confronting such tasks in your work situation without warning or consent in ways you dare not acknowledge or protest, for fear of losing your job. In addition, it can be very liberating to realize that other people's sexuality is not automatically your responsibility, a fact brought home when it becomes a task you do for pay.

My Advice to Naomi

Taking all this into account, I would indeed tell Naomi that she should consider taking the exotic dancer job, at least for the short term. Flatly put, it presents relatively low personal risk and gives her a good opportunity to improve her employment situation because of the shorter workday. A typical eight- to ten-hour workday, plus commuting time, would make it terribly difficult for her to pursue any sort of training or education that would prepare her for better work. This dynamic is particularly true of low-paid hourly wage jobs, where any need for more money translates into having less free time. Given that in either case Naomi is going to be exploited by an employer, and that in neither case will she be magically insulated from sexual objectification, the more ethical path, to me, is to take the job that offers better prospects for the future. Neither job offers particularly good prospects for a future *in that particular job*; they are called "dead-end jobs" for a reason. But one is a much more useful means to an end than the other.

At the same time, I would caution Naomi that not all sex work is created equal. Just as with "nonsexual" jobs, some employers and workplaces are better than others. I would encourage her to know her rights as an employee and learn about the laws in her state that affect sex work (what can be shown and whether patrons may touch dancers is often limited by law) to minimize legal risk. I would consider it a bonus if she were able to work in one of the small number of existing unionized or collectively run sex-work businesses, which offer better work conditions. And I would also encourage her to join one of several existing sex worker organizations for support and information. All these things would help Naomi protect herself from the potential problems of sex work, whether they be physical, legal, emotional, or social.

It is important that any employee limit his or her personal risk at work, while making the most of the benefits of his or her job. Because of this, I would advise Naomi against performing sex work that could potentially compromise her physical health (e.g., prostitution) or that would compromise her anonymity, like appearing in films or still photos. Phone sex work, on the other hand, is very safe and anonymous, and is a useful means of making a living, while leaving time open for other important pursuits.

My hope for Naomi in doing this work is that she would be able to enjoy it and use it for good ends, first for herself and then for expanding her economic/employment options. She might also, perhaps, use it to do good for other people. This side to sex work gets very little press, but it genuinely does exist. Many sex workers—including Jews like Annie Sprinkle and Carol Leigh, who coined the term "sex work"—have used sex work as a way to educate people about sexuality and sexual labor, and to combat gender and sex inequality. In a realm as full of injustices as that of sexuality, there is certainly much *tikkun*-oriented repair work to be done. Although it is not fair or reasonable to task Naomi with becoming the next sex-worker force for social justice, it is certainly reasonable to point out that the "sex worker" and the "social justice activist" can easily and usefully coexist, even within an individual. On a small scale, she might be able, for instance, to help other workers set up bank accounts, get access to job training, or hand out information about safer sex.

In closing, I want to emphasize that sex work is not without its drawbacks, but given the limitations imposed by sex/gender, sexism, heterosexism, socioeconomic class, and capitalism, it can be a valuable employment option. I do not believe that sex work is only valuable if it is a useful stepping-stone for getting out of sex work, even though it often is for many women. The sheer prevalence of sex work, and sexualized work, demonstrates that as a society we actually want and use a great deal more sexual labor than we acknowledge. The priorities of our capitalist patriarchy require that we refuse to see most of it, and that we condemn that which is too blatant to overlook. Until such time, however, as we are capable of acknowledging all sexual labor as "sex work" and treat all sexual laborers with respect and generosity reflective of their importance to the culture, sex industry workers are more likely than not to be best served by using sex work as strategically as possible as a means to another end.

Deconstructing the Commercial Sex Trade Industry
Rachel Durchslag and Aimee Dinschel

W HEN LOOKING at Naomi's current life situation, that of a 23-year-old female without a college education facing severely limited work options, it might appear that strip club work provides an attractive alternative to a minimum wage job. Based on the portrayals of strip clubs in films and music videos, many assume that stripping is an easy way to make large amounts of money with few negative consequences. We see HBO documentaries like *G-String Divas*, featuring women in the sex industry who praise the flexibility of working in a strip club, like the amount of money they make, and enjoy the feelings of empowerment they experience from being lusted after.

If strip clubs did, in fact, provide a positive work environment for women and allowed them agency over their working conditions, then choosing to do this work could be a viable option for Naomi. Yet for this to be true, we must assume the following: that most women working in strip clubs make large sums of money; that most of the money made in a strip club is from actual dancing; that Naomi will be able to have flexibility and negotiate her shifts and hours; and that the men who attend the club where she works will be respectful and nonviolent.

However, extensive research about the stripping industry and personal narratives from women who have worked at strip clubs challenge these presumptions.

Making Money
One of the biggest misconceptions about strip clubs, and one that Naomi's scenario reinforces, is that they offer women the opportunity to make large sums of money. Although it is true that some women do make substantial amounts of money during their time stripping, this is not the norm. Women in strip clubs are hired as independent contractors rather than as employees. Most are not paid a wage, and their income is dependent on their compliance to customers' demands in order to earn tips.

Women must also pay fees to work at clubs. These can include: providing money from tips to give to bouncers and disc jockeys, meeting nightly monetary quotas, and paying fines imposed by club management. Dancers can be fined $1 per minute for being late and as much as $100 for calling in sick. They may be charged fines for "talking back" to customers or staff, touching stage mirrors, using baby oil on stage, being late on stage, dancing with their back to a customer, or being touched by a customer. Additionally, Naomi's understanding of the type of work done in strip clubs is a typical misconception.

We have worked with survivors of the sex trade for the past five years. Many of the women we advocate for started working in strip clubs and entered into prostitution soon after. As Olivia Howard, a survivor of prostitution and an activist against sexual exploitation, explains:

> When you get to the strip club to work, you think you are actually hired as a dancer. But within two days you find out that the real money is being made by the number and types of drinks you sell. To move the guys from cocktails to Champagne bottles, the most expensive drink, means you have to go to the back room where prostitution acts occur. It only took me two weeks to figure this out. At the first club I worked at, the club owner set up a competition between the girls, and a bonus was given to those who sold the most expensive drinks. About 95% of women at the club eventually prostituted in the back room. Most of the time, the actual dancing on the stage and the loud music is a decoy, a distraction, from the prostitution occurring in the back.[1]

Club managers or owners also often encourage drug and alcohol use in order to keep the women dependent on stripping and, further, to ease them into prostitution. Though stripping may appear to be an easy way to make money, the dynamics of strip clubs are often much more complicated than just what the dancing entails, and the goal of management is for the owners, not the dancers, to walk away with the biggest profits.

Working Conditions

An appealing aspect of working at a strip club for Naomi is the opportunity to create her own hours and shift times. She thinks that a strip club is an environment where she can dictate her working conditions and schedule.

Though strip club work can offer some flexibility, this is not standard operating procedure. A good example is depicted in the film *Live*

---

1. Olivia Howard, interview by author, Chicago, Illinois, 6 January 2009.

Nude Girls Unite, where the women working at the Lusty Lady strip club talk about the challenges of taking days off or changing shifts. The club imposes strict rules governing the race and body type of the women dancing to ensure the most desirable mix. Therefore, if you are an African-American woman who wants a day off, you have to find an African-American woman with a similar body type to cover your shift. This can prove incredibly burdensome.[2]

Additionally, women in strip clubs often talk about how their relationship with the club can become all-consuming. As Olivia explains:

> For the first time in my life I felt that I was in control of my life. I had money, I could shop when I got ready, stay any place I wanted to, get an apartment here or there. You think, it is a sense of independence, but as it continues, it becomes a total dependent way of life.[3]

Being a dancer interferes with living a normal life. The long and late hours, tiredness, alcohol consumption, and out-of-town bookings make it difficult to have productive lives outside of the club.

Due to the verbal and physical harassment that are normal aspects of most strip clubs, women who strip often turn to substances as a way to dissociate from their experience. As Olivia states: "It is a myth that any woman can get up there and do that and not have something in her. It doesn't have to be hard-core drugs, but you have to take something to help you deal with it."[4] Many women start self-medicating with alcohol, and they transition to harder drugs easily. Some club owners actually provide drugs and alcohol as a way to have the dancers become more dependent on the club and more willing to perform sex acts in the champagne rooms.

Male Patrons of Strip Clubs

Often, women who work in strip clubs experience both physical and verbal abuse. Many dancers report that customers spit on them, flick them with cigarette butts, and pelt them with ice, trash, condoms, or bottles and

---

2. *Live Nude Girls Unite!*, DVD, directed by Vicki Funari and Julia Query (San Francisco, CA: First Run Features, 2000).
3. Jody Raphael, *Listening to Olivia: Violence, Poverty, and Prostitution* (Boston: Northeastern University Press, 2004), 54.
4. Ibid., 54.

cans. Strip club patrons also frequently grab dancers' breasts, buttocks, and genitals. Stories of patrons attempting and succeeding in penetrating strippers vaginally and anally with their fingers, dollar bills, bottles, and cell phones are common. Additionally, most clubs have private VIP rooms where dancers are alone with patrons. Behind these closed doors, abuse is common.

Another common experience that women face is being stalked. Customers follow women home, harass them at the clubs, and visit nightly in a manner that is intimidating. And even when women complain, management still expects them to greet and service these men if the customer is one of the club's big spenders.[5]

Though most physical wounds eventually heal, verbal abuse can leave emotional scars and psychological damage for a lifetime. One variable that Naomi may not be considering is what it is like to be called derogatory names on a daily basis by customers, owners, managers, and staff.

And even when physical and verbal abuse does not occur, there is an emotional impact from being consistently fondled and touched. Olivia explains:

Within thirty days the awful reality sets in. There are 50,000 hands touching me, you begin to feel dirty, the guys are smelly, they are usually drunk. Some of them sit and drink so much until they are physically sick. Even talking about it now, I can still smell them. That is the most disgusting part. They were animals.[6]

Even though Naomi says that she is not bothered by being objectified when stripping, there are broader implications for participating in an industry that reinforces notions of male entitlement to women's sexuality. Rape and sexual assault impact the lives of women and girls at alarming rates. In Illinois alone, it is estimated that there are at least 670,000 women who have experienced *forcible rapes* at some time in their lives, and those are only the sexual assaults that were reported to authorities; undoubtedly thousands more were raped but were too afraid or ashamed to report it.[7] Female bodies are continually commodified and used to sell

---

5. Howard, interview by author, January 6, 2009.
6. Raphael, 53.
7. Illinois General Assembly, House Resolution 1177, 2008, 2.

every type of product and service imaginable; there are even restaurants where you can eat food off of the body of a model.

At the same time that women's bodies are undergoing increased commodification, constructs of masculinity continue to incorporate messages that real men are sexually dominant and have easy sexual access to women. And so, a "rape culture" is created, where sexual violence against women is normalized and even condoned. One of the many harms of living in a "rape culture" is that women's bodies are not viewed as their own. Strip clubs further this notion by putting a price tag on women's sexuality, reinforcing the message that sexual access to women is a male entitlement.

Continuum of Exploitation: The Commercial Sex Trade Industry

Participating in the sex trade industry is not a moral issue but rather one of social justice. Women who enter into prostitution, phone sex, pornography, or other forms of the sex trade do so for very similar reasons. These include a lack of viable work options, feeding a substance addiction, fulfilling survival needs like food or shelter, or escaping a domestic violence situation. Most women enter the sex trade as a last resort, not as a first choice.

If we are going to use the word "morality" in this discussion, the most relevant question would be whether it is moral for men to patronize the sex trade, particularly when many of them know the negative life circumstances that draw women to prostitution. A man who purchases sex described the type of damaged women he expected to encounter:

> "I would imagine that prostitutes have had some sort of psychological and/or physical trauma as a child. Women who are prone to that sort of lifestyle are trying to repeat the cycles they encountered. Women who have been sexually molested."[8]

My organization, the Chicago Alliance Against Sexual Exploitation, worked in partnership with Prostitution Research and Education to interview 113 men who purchase sex. Many of our questions centered on how the men viewed women in the sex trade. Some men viewed

---

8. Rachel Durchslag and Samir Goswami, "Deconstructing the Demand for Prostitution: Preliminary Insights from Interviews with Chicago Men Who Purchase Sex," *Chicago Alliance Against Sexual Exploitation Independent Research*, May 2008, 20.

them as objects instead of as human beings: "I usually call for a girl, you know, like a pizza."[9] Other men thought that women engaged in prostitution actually have a different emotional makeup from other women: "They just have to have really low self-esteem and be numb on the inside, and be able to turn their emotions on and off."[10]

One of Naomi's questions is whether engaging in the sex trade industry might make her less desirable to a potential mate. Based on the answers provided by our interviewees, there is a good likelihood that men will not want to be romantically involved with Naomi if they know about her sex trade involvement: "You can't transfer a ho to a housewife."[11]

We asked men a variety of questions to further assess their attitudes about women engaged in prostitution. Below is an example of how men in our study feel about having a close relationship with someone in the sex trade:

- 85% would never marry a woman who had been involved in prostitution.
- 93% would not want their daughter to become a prostitute.
- 76% would not want their daughter to work in a strip club.
- 70% would not marry someone who had had sex for money.[12]

However, we maintain a double standard on accountability when it comes to understanding the sex trade industry. In many ways, our culture views purchasing sex as a male right. When I first decided to do research on the demand side of the sex trade, one of the motivating factors was the lack of research on the subject. There was an abundance of research investigating why women sell sex, but the number of studies about men purchasing sex in the United States was almost nonexistent. I believe one of the reasons that we do not analyze why men purchase sex is because we do not view it as something abnormal.

For some families, purchasing sex is seen as a right of passage. In our study, 17% of the men first purchased sex with a relative present. The experience was treated as a part of coming into manhood: "Like here is

9. Ibid., 16.
10. Ibid., 17.
11. Ibid., 19.
12. Ibid., 1–33.

your first sip of beer, here is your first hooker." Others viewed buying sex as a normative part of male behavior. These men viewed prostitution as something natural and even beneficial to individuals and society. 95% asserted that prostitution would always exist, 63% claimed that most men go to prostitutes once in a while, and 52% thought that it would be fine if their son visited a brothel.[13]

What is the Solution?

There are countless women who are in situations similar to Naomi's. The question should not be whether or not they should enter the commercial sex trade. The question is why there are such limited options for women to make a living wage.

If we want real solutions, we need to focus our efforts on providing viable economic opportunities for women, ensuring access to substance abuse counseling and safe shelters for women, preventing childhood sexual abuse, and confronting institutions that normalize sexual violence and sexual exploitation. As a man in our study indicated: "Prostitution would stop if we could stop molestation, economics, forcing children into sex, and domination by men."[14]

Equally as important, we need to prevent men from patronizing the sex trade and intervene with those currently purchasing sex. As long as there is a demand to purchase sex, vulnerable individuals will continue to be recruited and harmed in systems of sexual exploitation. When asking those who purchase sex what the solution to this problem is, one man aptly responded: "If there were no customers, there would be no prostitution."[15]

---

13. Ibid., 14.
14. Ibid., 24.
15. Ibid., 24.

Sex Work: Whose Choice?

Martha Ackelsberg

QUESTIONS ABOUT the ethics of "sex work" (I include working at strip clubs, prostitution, and pornography underneath that term) are endlessly fascinating and confusing. Many of my students at an elite women's college, for example, seem to believe that a woman's ability to freely "choose" to work as a stripper or prostitute, without being degraded or demeaned for that choice, is one of the signal achievements of feminism. Feminism, they argue, is about autonomy and freedom, the right of women to use their bodies just as freely as men do.

Others, notably feminists Andrea Dworkin and Catharine MacKinnon, argue that such work is never really *freely* chosen; and, even if it were or could be, it should not be chosen because it contributes to the objectification and degradation of women. From the point of view of Kantian ethics—the view that people should be treated as ends in themselves, not as means to the achievement of others' ends—sex work treats women as *means* (for men to achieve some degree of titillation or sexual satisfaction through the use of women's bodies) and is, therefore, unacceptable.

From a Jewish point of view, we could argue that the objectifications entailed in sex work effectively deny the respect and dignity that women ought to be accorded as beings created in the image of God.

So how should a contemporary Jewish feminist counsel Naomi to approach the choices she confronts?

I believe that the first, and most important, step in dealing with this situation is to recognize that ethical decision-making involves not just *individual* choices made in a vacuum, but the *context* in which one's choices are made. To me, that is one of the great contributions and lessons of Jewish tradition. We live in communities; these communities structure the opportunities to which we have access, and it is the responsibility of the community to work toward equality and dignity for all. In the words of the prophet Isaiah, who chided the Israelites for fasting while ignoring the real needs of people in the community:

Is such the fast I desire,
A day for people to starve their bodies?
Is it bowing the head like a bulrush ...?
No, this is the fast I desire:

105

To unlock the fetters of wickedness,
And untie the cords of the yoke
To let the oppressed go free;
To break off every yoke.
It is to share your bread with the hungry,
And to take the wretched poor into your home;
When you see the naked, to clothe him .... (Isa. 58: 5–7)

If we do *not* take context into account, then any attempt to address stripping under the terms posed for us will be impossible. We are encouraged to interpret the dilemma as if it were simply Naomi's problem: Does she choose the drugstore job because it is less exploitative of her and others, and therefore, the more "moral" option? Or does she choose to work as a stripper because she will make more money and be more able to control her hours of work? Emma Goldman, an early 20th-century anarchist and feminist, used a character from George Bernard Shaw's play *Mrs. Warren's Profession* to put the question quite starkly: "With Mrs. Warren these girls feel, 'Why waste your life working for a few shillings a week in a scullery, eighteen hours a day?'" if they could make good money as prostitutes?[1]

Posed in this way, the ethical questions are *Naomi's* problem: Should *she* contribute to the commodification and objectification of women's bodies by participating in this work? Should *she* attempt to insist on certain working conditions? What is the most moral choice? As feminist political philosopher Carole Pateman has noted with respect to prostitution, however,

> "the ... assumption that prostitution is a problem about women ensures that the other participant in the prostitution contract escapes scrutiny. [But] ... prostitution can be seen as a problem about *men*. The problem of prostitution then becomes encapsulated in the question why men demand that women's bodies are sold as commodities in the capitalist market."[2]

Similarly, to pose the questions only for Naomi is to ignore the larger framework: What does it mean that we live in a society in which

---

1. Emma Goldman, "The Traffic in Women" in *Anarchism and Other Essays* (New York: Dover Press, 1969). Available at http://womenshistory.about.com/library/etext/bl_eg_an8_traffic_in_women.htm.
2. Carole Pateman, "What's Wrong with Prostitution?" in *The Sexual Contract* (Stanford, CA: Stanford University Press, 1988), 193, 194.

strippers are paid better than drugstore clerks (or day care workers, or home health aides, or many teachers!)? What is the responsibility of everyone else (not least those who take advantage of the "services" of strippers, prostitutes, and other sex workers) who upholds, and benefits from, a society that manifests those values? In what sense can we say that the "choice" to work as a stripper (or as a prostitute) in such a context is, truly, a *free* choice, or even a choice at all?

In the end, I want to argue that no one should have to choose between selling her—or his—body and being able to support her or himself at a reasonable level. At the same time, I also do not want to say that, under the circumstances Naomi confronts, she should not "choose" to be a stripper. Rather, I think the more appropriate and more compelling ethical questions are about *how* the choices she has came to be her choices, and what responsibilities the rest of us have for those choices.

Let me begin by saying something about what I take the "choice" of being a stripper to entail. The case proposes to us that "she could earn significant money for minimal hours' work, and…[would have] more flexibility to negotiate her shifts and her hours." It goes on to say that Naomi "regards sex work as, simply, a form of physical labor," even though she recognizes that "her work contributes to the objectification of women, generally." But the picture this paints of the freedom and autonomy of sex work is, in fact, much too rosy. Strip clubs are a multi-billion dollar business in the U.S., and most of those billions are not going to the strippers themselves! More to the point, being a dancer in a strip club generally requires that the stripper do much more than dance on a stage—at the least, she is expected to be willing to be "groped," to participate in "champagne rooms" with clients, and, even more likely, to engage in lap dancing, or, in some cases, in more explicit forms of sex.

Further, although being a stripper is often considered to be safer and "cleaner" than being a prostitute, strippers may be pressured into prostitution (or, at the very least, into engaging in various kinds of sex-related activities) in order to pay their "rent" for dancing at the club. Thus, considerable coercion may well be involved even in a situation where a woman believes she has freely entered into a contract.[3]

---

3. See, for example, the report of a raid on a series of strip clubs in Seattle, "Police and Feds Raid Colacurcio Strip Clubs," *Seattle Post-Intelligencer*, June 3, 2008. Available at http://seattlepi.nwsource.com/local/365475_strip03.html.

In short, strip-dancing does not necessarily allow the stripper the autonomy it promises, and it is also potentially quite dangerous.

Of course, one could make the argument that there is no significant difference between selling one's body—whether as a stripper or as a prostitute—and other forms of work. All workers "sell themselves" to some degree. That is why low-wage employment has often been referred to as "wage slavery." At the other end of the spectrum, rock stars, film stars, and sports figures also sell their bodies, and get quite well-paid for doing so!

But there *is* a difference between sex work and other, more traditional, forms of wage labor. Although workers use their bodies to perform their jobs, they do not make the whole of their bodies available to (invasion by) their employers, at the discretion of those employers. As Carole Pateman has put it, a traditional employer "is primarily interested in the commodities produced by the worker," while, for the one who engages the services of a stripper or of a prostitute, "the body of the woman, and sexual access to that body, is the subject of the contract."[4] Thus, sex work is not only demeaning to women (even if the women are relatively highly paid); it also reinforces the overall subordination (and, in particular, the *sexual* subordination) of women by reinforcing and validating the belief that men have an interest in, and a right to, sexual access to women's bodies.

Alternatively, one could also say (along with Emma Goldman) that, in a context where women cannot find other decently-paid "legitimate" work by which to support themselves, and therefore turn to marriage to assure their survival, there is really no difference between marriage and prostitution: "it is merely a question of degree whether she sells herself to one man, in or out of marriage, or to many men."[5] Goldman made that comparison, however, *not* in order to argue that women *ought* to choose prostitution; but, rather, to make evident, and condemn, the hypocrisy and self-righteousness of those who criminalized the prostitute without attending to the larger context in which prostitution took place. Who can blame women, she asked, if selling their bodies is the only way to keep themselves and their children fed and out of the cold? Instead, we should focus our attention on the economic system that denies many workers (and especially poorly-educated women) access to decent jobs at livable wages.

---

4. Pateman, "What's Wrong with Prostitution?," 203.
5. Emma Goldman, "The Traffic in Women."

Similarly, although the questions in the case study are posed as questions of *individual* morality ("Should she ... take the job only under certain working conditions?" "If she had more economic and professional options ... are there reasons she should not choose this?"), I think it is wrong and misleading to treat them as such. Whether she should or should not take the job based on some abstract standards of morality is not really the important ethical question here. As a feminist Jew who values the dignity of all human lives, I believe that people should not be forced to place themselves in dangerous situations in order to make enough money to survive. If she were to take the job, Naomi would certainly be best off if she could insist that she would not have to engage in unwanted sexual acts with customers, that she would not be fondled or groped without her permission, etc. But those kinds of "conditions" are precisely what are not likely to be negotiable in the contract Naomi will have to sign (if she has one at all!).

To put this another way: Naomi's "choices" are very limited. She is not setting the terms of employment, but she must choose what seems best in a structure that is not organized according to her needs and has no concern for what is good for her. Only if the world (and U.S. society) were differently structured—if there were sufficiently attractive alternatives available—could we treat her decision about whether to work as a stripper (or as a prostitute, or even to offer phone sex) as a question simply about her "freedom" to use her body as she chooses. In the absence of that fundamental change, however, I do not think these questions have easily discernable answers.

Rather, the more significant ethical issues are those confronting the rest of us: a) the patrons or consumers of strip clubs, pornography, or prostitution; b) those who own such establishments; and, not insignificantly, c) all those who may neither patronize nor derive profits from these establishments, but, nevertheless, live in a society where too many people are forced into "choosing" these kinds of jobs because they can find no viable alternatives.

a) **Patrons.** I do think that there is a *significant* moral difference between engaging in this work as a stripper or prostitute and being the patron of a sex worker. The former is trying to survive, the latter is enacting some fantasy of male domination/female subordination. As Pateman notes, claims that men "need" to patronize such establishments because sex, like food, is a "natural human urge" are patently false.

While people die for lack of food (or shelter), no one (to my knowledge, at least) has died for lack of sex! Moreover, Pateman points out that all these institutions reinforce the idea of male sex-right, that men have some sort of "natural" right of access to women's bodies. A male client's desire for access to women's bodies is not just about the satisfaction of an "urge": How else, Pateman wonders, would we explain that "15 to 25% of the customers of Birmingham prostitutes demand what is known in the trade as 'hand relief'?"[6]

b) **Profiteers.** Further, there is an even greater distinction between workers in the sex industry and the owners of the establishments in which they work. For the most part, the workers are poorly paid, frequently demeaned, and subject to violence and harassment. The owners, on the other hand, are participating in a multi-billion dollar business that is based entirely on exploitation—both of its workers and of those who patronize their establishments. Their success is predicated on the overall societal subordination of women, and it contributes to maintaining that subordination, while relying on the relative lack of well-paying alternative employment for women. There can be, it seems to me, no moral justification for engaging in that particular form of "entrepreneurship."

c) **Society at Large.** This leaves the rest of us, who may think we are free of any responsibility if we avoid such establishments. But here is where, I believe, Jewish and anarchist/feminist traditions join in offering us a further challenge. No one has "clean hands" in a society where some are effectively forced into sex work by the lack of viable alternatives. If our concerns are for the ethics of people's employment choices, then our first priority should be to work for better, and more widely available education; for decent jobs that allow workers to support themselves and their families; for more egalitarian social and economic structures; and for a set of social practices that embody respect for all persons and challenge the assumption that women's bodies are created for men's pleasure.

Until we have succeeded in creating such a society, "choices" about sex work are rightly on the consciences of all of us.

---

6. Pateman, "What's Wrong with Prostitution?," 199.

CASE 4

❧

SEXUAL NEGOTIATION

Case Study

JIM AND SARAH are married, with two children, ages 3 and 1. Although they have a happy marriage, there are some sexual issues that they have to work out. Sarah's sexual appetite is generally a bit stronger than Jim's, and she has sexual interests that are not exciting or appealing to Jim—and vice-versa.

On a given evening, if one partner wants to have sex and the other does not, does the disinterested partner have an obligation to acquiesce to the sexual needs of the other partner? What if this is an ongoing issue in which one partner habitually wants sex and the other does not? To what extent is sexual accommodation an obligation in Jewish law? Does that matter?

Sarah is most sexually aroused when she is spanked. Jim is deeply uncomfortable with this; he thinks that it is demeaning to her and does not like the idea of hitting her, even when requested. Does Jim have an obligation to fulfill Sarah's request? Does his obligation change if this is the only way that Sarah can come to orgasm?

Should Jim or Sarah, as an act of caring for the other, agree to engage in any of the following: cuddling; oral sex (giving or receiving); spanking or being spanked; anal sex (giving or receiving); using degrading language (giving or receiving); watching pornography together before sex; tying the other up or agreeing to be tied up; erotic role-playing; cross-dressing; engaging in S/M (sado-masochistic sex); engaging in a ménage à trois?

If you were to draw a line as to what is and is not acceptable, why would you draw that line and where would you draw it?

Traditional Sources

Compiled by Uzi Weingarten and the Editors

On the Duties of Spouses to Each Other

1. Mishnah, *Avot* (Pirkei Avot) 5:19

When love depends on achieving a certain goal, love vanishes when that goal is achieved; but a love that does not depend on any goal never vanishes.

2. Exodus 21:10

If he marries another, he must not withhold from this one her food, her clothing, or her conjugal rights.

Note: The Hebrew word for conjugal rights, *onah*, is literally understood by the Rabbis as "duration," referring to conjugal relations and the frequency thereof; some biblical scholars translate the word as "ointments."

3. Mishnah, *Ketubbot* 5:6

If a man put his wife under a vow to have no connubial intercourse, the School of Shammai says [that he may continue to maintain the vow] for two weeks, but the School of Hillel says [that he may do so] only for one week. Students may leave their wives at home to study Torah without their wives' permission for thirty days; laborers for one week. The time for marital duties enjoined in the Torah are: for men of independent means every day; for workmen twice weekly; for ass-drivers once a week; for camel-drivers once every thirty days; for sailors once every six months. This is the opinion of Rabbi Eliezer.

4. Maimonides (Rambam), *Mishneh Torah*, Laws of Marriage 12:7–8

7. One may not deny his wife her *onah*. If he denied her in order to cause her emotional pain, he transgresses a Torah prohibition, as it is written: "He may not diminish her food, her clothing and her *onah*" (Exodus 21:10). If he is unable to have sexual intercourse ... he either receives her permission or grants her a divorce and pays her *ketubbah*."

8. A woman who denies her husband sexual intercourse is called rebellious.

On the Modes of Sexual Intercourse
5. Babylonian Talmud, *Nedarim* 20b

R. Yochanan said ... our Sages said: A man may do whatever he pleases with his wife [during intercourse]. A parable: meat that comes from the butcher may be eaten salted, roasted, cooked or seethed; so too with fish from the fishmonger.

6. Maimonides (Rambam), *Mishneh Torah*, Laws of Forbidden Intercourse 21:9, 12

9. All that a man wishes to do with his wife he may do ... He may kiss any part of her and have intercourse "as is her way" and "not as is her way" (i.e., vaginally and anally, respectively).

12. The Sages forbade a man from having sexual intercourse [with this wife] while thinking about another woman, or when drunk, or when quarreling [with her], or when in hatred [of her]; and he should not have sex with her coercively, with her afraid of him.

7. Nahmanides (Ramban), Letter of Holiness (*Iggeret ha-Kodesh*), Chapter 6

You ought to engage her first in matters that please her heart and mind and cheer her in order to bring together your thought with her thought and your intention with hers. And you should say such things, some of which will urge her to passion and intercourse, to affection, desire and love-making, and some which will urge fear of heaven, piety and modesty. You should attract her with charming words and seductions and other proper and righteous things, as I have explained. And do not possess her while she is asleep because the two intentions are not one and her wish does not agree with yours ... Finally ... do not hasten to arouse your passion until the woman's mind is ready, and engage her in words of love.

On Homosexual Relations
8. Leviticus 18:22

Do not lie with a male as one lies with a woman; it is an abhorrence.

9. Leviticus 20:13

If a man lies with a male as one lies with a woman, the two of them have done an abhorrent thing; they shall be put to death—their bloodguilt is upon them.

10. Babylonian Talmud, *Sanhedrin* 54a–54b

Our Rabbis taught: "If a man lies with a male ..." (Leviticus 20:13): "A man" excludes a minor; "who lies with a male" denotes either an adult or a minor; "as a man lies with a woman" teaches that there are two modes of intimacy [anal and vaginal], both of which are punished when committed as an act of incest.... This [verse] teaches the punishment; from where do we learn the formal prohibition for him who lies [with a male]— that is, from where do we know a formal prohibition for the person who permits himself to be thus sexually involved? Scripture says, "There shall be no cult prostitute (*kadesh*) of the sons of Israel" (Deuteronomy 23:18) ...; this is Rabbi Ishmael's view. Rabbi Akiba said: [Deriving the prohibition from that verse] is unnecessary, for one can read [the unvoweled Hebrew text of Leviticus 18:22, as it appears in the Torah as both] "Do not lie with a male as one lies with a woman" and "Do not be lain with."

11. Babylonian Talmud, *Nedarim* 51a

Bar Kappara asked Rabbi [Judah, President of the Sanhedrin]: What is the meaning of *to'evah* (abomination, as in Leviticus 18:22, the verse banning homosexual relations)? He then refuted every explanation offered by Rabbi. "Explain it yourself," Rabbi then said. Bar Kappara replied: ... Thus the All Merciful One said: *to'evah* = *to'eh ata bah* [you go astray in respect to it. He is using a play on words, for this phrase in Hebrew sounds like the Hebrew word for abomination].

12. Maimonides (Rambam), *Mishneh Torah*, Laws of Forbidden Intercourse 21:8

Women who rub one against the other—this is forbidden. It is among the acts of Egypt against which we were warned, for it says (Leviticus 18:3): "You shall not copy the practices of the land of Egypt." The Sages said (Sifra, Aharei Mot, 9:8): "What is it that they would do? A man would marry a man, a woman would marry a woman, or a woman would marry two men." Even though this practice is prohibited, one does not receive lashes, for there is no specific biblical prohibition and it is not called "intercourse" at all. Therefore, they are not prohibited [subsequently from marrying] into the priesthood on account of licentiousness, and a woman is not prohibited to her husband on account of this ... But it is appropriate to give them lashes [on rabbinic authority] for rebelliousness, since they have done a prohibited thing.

Contemporary Sources

Compiled by Steven Edelman-Blank

1. Shmuley Boteach, *Kosher Sex: A Recipe for Passion and Intimacy* (New York: Doubleday, 1999), 84

The definition of holiness in sex is anything that serves to bring a husband and a wife closer together. Barriers that separate a husband and wife should always be avoided.

The religious wife in the story that began this chapter has, of course, every right to refrain from oral sex if it is something she personally feels uncomfortable with, and a husband should never push his wife to anything that repels her. But that still doesn't mean that he can't try, lovingly, to persuade her about doing things that will bring them mutual pleasure. Yet neither spouse should base their objections to a sexual position on piety, because religion desires husbands and wives to be totally satisfied with each other sexually. Far from being an exalted level of piety, prudishness in marriage is a sin that might push spouses to explore, either directly or through fantasy, possibilities outside the marriage.

2. Marla Brettschneider, "Questing for Heart in a Heartless World: Jewish Feminist Ruminations on Monogamy and Marriage," in *The Family Flamboyant: Race Politics, Queer Families, Jewish Lives* (Albany, NY: SUNY Press, 2006), 133

In the expectations and promises of monogamous marriage the present is lost, and relation becomes an object with a pretense to the future as real. For [philosopher Martin] Buber this is a stultifying of the present. It is not the aliveness promised by the ideological vision, but instead "cessation, suspension, a breaking off and cutting clear and hardening, absence of relation and of being present."

3. Jay Michaelson, *God in Your Body: Kabbalah, Mindfulness and Embodied Spiritual Practice* (Woodstock, Vermont: Jewish Lights Publishing, 2007), 64–65

For instance, there are at least two ways to read the Talmudic edict that a man must make love to his wife every day, unless under certain circumstances. One is to read the rule as being about husband and wife. Another is to translate the sex-positive injunction into the meaningful relationships we hold today. Just as the Talmudic Rabbis required frequent, healthy sexual activity within their world, so should we in ours.

4. Michael Strassfeld, *A Book of Life: Embracing Judaism as a Spiritual Practice* (New York: Schocken Books, 2002), 370

The Reconstructionist and then the Reform movement have taken a position that affirms homosexuality. They have ordained gay and lesbian rabbis, and some rabbis in both movements will perform same-sex commitment ceremonies (the equivalents of marriages). These policies reflect a larger attitude that no longer sees homosexuality as wrong, but rather as another form of human sexuality. They suggest that our attitude has changed from that of the Bible, just as it has on other issues such as slavery and the status of women. For some this change in attitude has to do with evidence that suggests homosexuality is not a choice but part of the genetic makeup of some people. For others, it reflects an understanding that relations between homosexuals are no different from those between heterosexuals. At their best, they are relations of deep love and commitment. This is also part of an expanded definition of what constitutes families. For me, the affirmation of homosexuality follows from all that I have already said about sexuality. There is an opportunity to experience holiness through the intimacy between two people. Since sex for Judaism is not just about having children, I would suggest that the Talmud's statements that permit any act that both people want to be expanded to include two adults of the same sex. Ultimately homosexuality and heterosexuality should be seen as aspects of the same Divine desire: "it is not good for a human to be alone."

5. Elliot N. Dorff, Daniel S. Nevins and Avram Reisner. Summary of "Homosexuality, Human Dignity and Halakhah," a rabbinic ruling for the Conservative Movement, September 2006. Available at http://www.rabbinicalassembly.org/docs/Dorff_paper.pdf

The tension between our traditional sexual norms and our contemporary understanding of sexual orientation has created a complicated dilemma for both Jewish homosexuals and for the entire Torah observant community. We have approached this difficult subject with humility and reverence, and have come to the following understanding: A review of the biblical and rabbinic sources reveals that only one form of homosexual intimacy, anal intercourse between men, is explicitly forbidden by the Torah. Other forms of homosexual intimacy between men and between women have been prohibited by the authority of the Rabbis.

As our understanding of sexual orientation has evolved, so too has our sensitivity to the horrific effects of the halakhah's comprehensive ban on the sexual behavior of Torah observant homosexuals. They have no legal options for sexual and social intimacy within the traditional parameters. This situation is degrading and even dangerous for them. Yet the halakhah also teaches its practitioners to be zealous in protecting human dignity. The [Talmudic] principle *gadol kvod habriot shedocheh lo ta'aseh sheba Torah* [respect for the dignity of people is so great that it can trump a negative Torah commandment] (Brakhot 19b etc.), has been applied in the Talmud and Codes of Halakhah in order to supersede rabbinic prohibitions for the sake of human dignity. We believe that the halakhic status quo violates the dignity of gay and lesbian Jews, and we propose the supersession of the rabbinic prohibitions on homosexual sex for the sake of human dignity.

6. Hanne Blank, "The 'Big O' Also Means 'Olam' " in *Yentl's Revenge: The Next Wave of Jewish Feminism*," Danya Ruttenberg, ed. (Seattle, WA: Seal Press, 2001), 200, 201

Negotiating the holiness and value we know to exist in our sexuality and our lives—as unmarried people, bisexuals, gays, lesbians, transsexuals—through Judaism's traditional blindness to nonheterosexual, nonmarital sexuality is a damned tough job.

One way to do this is to look to traditional Jewish law and customs for models for relationships, loves and sexualities that are not traditional. For instance, in Jewish law, a married man is obligated to give his wife a certain amount of sexual pleasure, or *onah*, per week or month as part of his side of the bargain in taking care of her needs as his spouse. A polyamorous couple—two people who have chosen not to be monogamous, but who openly and responsibly maintain other relationships in addition to their relationship to one another—struggling with ways to honor the primary relationship might well benefit from using this structure; the couple might decide that the primary commitment would benefit from being given *onah* and commit to a certain number of nights spent together each week...

People practicing BDSM [bondage, discipline, and sado-masochism] might conceptualize negotiations—who takes on what role(s), what acts are and are not acceptable, what parameters of sexual and other activity are to be part of their interactions with one another—as a form of *ketubah*, or marriage contract, specifying what each partner is obligated to bring to the relationship and what each can expect in terms of support and help if things go poorly.

Responses

Negotiating Orgasm: Spirituality and the Sexual Experience

Gabriel Blau

ONE SATURDAY in 2002, I was having a fairly typical night for a young single gay man in New York. I was at a small club downtown where the latest remix of the dance song *du jour* was playing so loudly that it was impossible to talk over it. The place was packed. I was wearing my *kippah,* as I always did back then.

Wearing a *kippah* at a gay bar or club always meant a portion of the evening would be spent listening to people's stories about growing up, finding God, leaving God, and still thinking about God. People would tell me about their trips to Israel, the shul they grew up in, their former life as a religious person, and so forth. I only wish I had been able to record all of those conversations; the stories were priceless. They told of their deep desire to reclaim their faith, or to destroy it completely. On this night, however, one such interaction would take up permanent residence in my memory and forever inform my own sexuality and spirituality.

I found myself in the bathroom (for totally wholesome reasons). Next to me, a curly-haired man about my age, fairly inebriated, spotted my *kippah* and said, "I'm Jewish too! Look!" He started unzipping his pants.

"No, No, NO. I believe you! Really. I think you may have had a little too much to drink…," I said trying to be cool, calm, responsible, and yet maintain my charm (I was, after all, single. And he was, after all, Jewish). But he persisted, and to my great surprise showed me not his penis, but a two-inch blue Jewish star tattoo on his right thigh.

This man at the club in New York made a permanent mark that would declare to every sexual partner he was ever with—whether for a night or a lifetime—that he had a God. He chose to combine two of the most powerful impulses humans have.

Spiritual Seduction

In order to negotiate sexual relationships, we must first recognize the deep spirituality and power of sex itself. Sex and sexuality are deeply spiritual and powerful regardless of our own awareness of these qualities.

121

Negotiating sexual relationships requires recognition of the inherently present connections between sex and the spirit. And to find them, we should not look only at texts and law, but also to the human experience.

At the center of every great prayer experience that I have ever had, there has been a profound yearning, a desire that is strong and alluring, yet mysterious and elusive. The greatest of our tradition's liturgy and music offer us a sense of awe, empowerment, and release. These are the same qualities present in our sexual desires and experiences. Like prayer, they can be ecstatic, yet like prayer they can, at times, also be off-putting and demeaning. Both spiritual practice, in all of its forms (some of which are sexual), and sex offer opportunities for unique connections to others and to ourselves. They require faith and trust, and they have a presence in our lives that can seem limited to isolated occasions, yet are part of almost everything we see and feel.

Spiritual journeys are replete with seduction and ecstatic moments. (I define spirituality here as our emotional and intellectual relationship with our faith, and our beliefs about the meaning of life [and death], a higher presence on this earth, and our roles in a story greater than ourselves.) Indeed, when one thinks about the experience of the "spiritual" and the experience of sex (seeking it, having it, negotiating it, remembering it), the same terms often come to mind: desire, freedom, ecstasy, boundaries, exploration, passion, confusion, mystery, connection, fear, joy.

The best sex, I think, is simultaneously greedy and giving. And what is prayer, but the act of giving God due appreciation and praise, and seeking more? One of my teachers described the *Amidah* prayer as a child standing with her arms outstretched and saying, "Give me." And in a way, it is the most beautiful and honest interaction we have with God. The whole prayer service is a balance of thinking about God, about ourselves, about needs and wants, and about sacrifice. That is, essentially, what sex is: the basic structure is often the same, yet each time is a different experience because the level of fulfillment can vary, and one's needs can suddenly change. Sometimes it is a long, quiet, and intimate experience of the senses. Sometimes it is about getting something done (or over with), and sometimes it is about ecstatic energies. This is the spiritual struggle—the path of the devoted and skeptical alike—that requires us to regularly revisit our needs, our obligations, our shortcomings, and our strengths.

The Questions We Ask and the Answers We Seek

When I first started grappling with my sexuality and what it meant to be a Gay Jew, all of my questions centered on Jewish law. May I do this or not? Does God want me to or not? Is anal sex okay or not? Is oral sex okay or not? Though those questions can have broad theological meaning, my inquiry was simpler: I wanted to know if Leviticus 18:22 and 20:13 meant that being and living as a Gay Jew was defying God.

As a college freshman, I was conflicted, upset, angry, and hurt. I was out to the world and to my family, but my faith posed challenges. God, Torah, and the Jewish community, to all of which I had dedicated myself, had left me feeling alone, had denied my legitimacy, and had caused me too many sleepless nights. My boyfriend at the time asked me a single question: What do you want to see happen?

Perhaps I might have said, "I want vindication, acceptance, equality." Instead, in a moment of unusual clarity, I answered, "I want to see intelligent people speak intelligently about sexuality and God." That was the beginning of the God & Sexuality Conference.

Though it sounded open-ended and exploratory, the meaning of my statement was specific: I wanted an answer to the verses in Leviticus that seemed to outlaw sex between men and, in some readings, prohibited all aspects of homosexuality. I wanted an irrefutable argument on the issue that would set everyone straight (in a manner of speaking).

My questions were all legal in nature. I was asking about Dos and Don'ts. I recognized my desires, but I sought answers that were concrete and explicit and that vindicated my own feelings. I had been set in this direction by both my own belief (at the time) that Judaism is legally based and comes down to doing God's will, and by the first rabbi I came out to, who asked, "What are you going to do about Leviticus?" Leviticus? I did not know about Leviticus. I thought my problems with Judaism would be cultural, a lack of presence in our scripture and history. I thought I would just be fighting run-of-the-mill bigotry—the type in which people hate me for no good reason, don't understand me, or just haven't been exposed to gay people and/or perspectives. I expected the regular stuff that got people exiled from their communities, disowned, and subjected to physical harm. And because I was in what I thought of as a fairly liberal community, I assumed that, at most, I would have to be somewhat of a trailblazer. But now, it seemed, the homophobia I would encounter had God on its side!

One of the first questions I was ever asked at a public forum was whether or not I had anal sex. Just a few minutes earlier I had explained at great length the literal meaning and traditional interpretations of Leviticus 18:22 and 20:13. Then, in a moment of naïveté, I opened up for questions with, "Ask me anything." So they did. But the man who asked this particular question did not care about the kind of sex I have. What he sought was guidance on what might be allowed. He had heard, it came out in private conversation later, the interpretations of the Torah. What he was looking for was what people really do.

Part of discovering and exploring one's connection to God and Torah is using models, examples of faith and devotion. Our literary history is a collection of, on one-hand, rules and instructions, and on the other, models for their observance (and warnings about transgressions).

We tell and retell stories of studying Torah (the Rabbis of Bnai Brak as told in the Passover haggadah), being kind (Abraham and Sarah opening their home to strangers), being unkind (Miriam and Aaron gossiping about their brother Moses), being devoted (Isaac's willingness to follow his father to the altar), and so on. From the Creation in Genesis to the journey of the Exodus, to the Rabbis of the Talmud, Jews have maintained and cultivated a vast library of examples. But there are still areas where the guidance feels thin. And when it comes to issues of sex and partnership, all the models in the world do not help much if you feel that none of those models was designed for you or your relationship.

So here is a new list of questions for Jim and Sarah:

Do you enjoy sex with each other?
Is your relationship fulfilling?
Has your sex life changed?
Did you have sex with other people before you met?
Do you masturbate?
Have you tried the things you now want (or don't want)?
How do you feel when you are asked to do something sexually that you do not like?
How do you feel when you share what you want from your partner? When you keep what you want from your partner?
How do you feel when your partner rejects your sexual requests?
Why do you need this now?
Why do you not feel you can give your partner what she or he wants?

The questions we ask and the answers we seek are fundamentally tied to our understanding of what should and could be in a sexual relationship. We grow up with a lot of images of sex acts. What we lack are representations of the deeper issues around sexual needs.

Jim and Sarah

I read through the list of potential acts Jim and Sarah might consider and wanted to say, "Yes, yes, yes! Go for it!" If that is what your partner is into, go ahead, make it happen, see where it takes you. But that kind of carefree attitude is a political response, a desire to encourage a world of exploration and discovery of the ways we can be intimate.

We should each strive to please our partners, but at what point do we risk alienating them? Sarah's desire to be spanked is about more than getting off, and Jim's reason for denying her request may be reasonable. But we are not talking about movie choices, or what to have for dinner. Sharing a sexual desire with your partner is a serious revelation. We do not know ahead of time what other people "are into" or what they might find acceptable. We do not know if other people are having anal sex, or spanking each other, or are refusing such sexual expressions. Our culture encourages us to generalize to the point of discomfort when it comes to our real personal preferences.

The questions we ask should include ones of the "deeper" variety—not because we must each elevate all sex to the spiritual, but because sex is already spiritual, even when just for physical enjoyment, even when we do not recognize the connection, and because tapping into our own spiritual selves can make sex so much better.

In any form, at any time, with anyone, sex is more than a collection of acts. It is about giving and taking, desire, enjoyment, gratitude, selfishness and selflessness. The greatest sexual expressions of love are a delicate balance of selfish animal desire and an intense need to give to your partner. Who would be fulfilled without both partners being desirous and present?

Jim and Sarah are not unique. Negotiations of boundaries, give and take, and responsibilities are inherent in a sexual relationship, as in all aspects of any relationship. But our culture makes it particularly hard to address sexual issues. It is not that we fail to talk about sex or about sexuality. We talk about it all the time now. We read about it. We watch other people have sex. What we do not do is talk about the negotiations, and especially not our own negotiations.

Acts of sex can be everything from cold and calculated to comforting and intimate. But surrounding sex is a complex web of negotiation of needs, desires, fantasies, and ego. We negotiate these issues within ourselves as well as with our partners. What, when, why, and how we like the kind of sex we like tends to be a secret we each keep for ourselves. And to complicate matters, most of us are unaware of the complexity of our own sexual needs.

Seeking spiritual fulfillment once one is exposed to its glory becomes a deeply personal process. Even though sexual fulfillment is usually experienced with a partner, that sense of fulfillment is about the person's own process and needs. Your partner can offer physical and verbal pleasure, but accepting those offerings as fulfilling depends on how you process them and what you need. You may not be able to change your own spiritual and physical needs, but you are the best one to attempt that job.

How we integrate our Judaism, God, and spirit into the negotiation process is less a matter of adding to that process, and more a matter of recognizing that it occurs. The spirit is there. Our decisions are not made in a vacuum. There are Jewish laws, there are cultural norms, there are personal preferences. Our desires are thus not singly drawn from a need for orgasm, and there is no single list of the good and bad ways of enjoying sex. Sex can make someone feel powerful, wonderful, ashamed, small, loved, hated, and even divine.

Sacred Sexuality

I asked a colleague about his relationship with his partner. I read him the case study for this essay and asked what he thought. He said very simply, "There is nothing my partner could request that I would not be willing to try. I trust her completely, and short of a few illegal things, I would be happy to learn new ways of fulfilling her needs."

That is trust. But that is also rare, at least in practice. If we each remember that sex is sacred, no matter when and how you have it, we can begin to come to a better place with our partners.

I think back to that curly-haired, tattooed man in 2002. He had created a literal, physical connection between his spiritual roots and his sexual desires through his tattoo. I do not know him, and I never had a chance to talk with him, but in my mind he has chosen to make a powerful statement that will always be with him and his partners, and that brings the spirit into sex every time. When he has sex, it is always amid something greater, and hopefully, as a result, the sex is greater too.

Sex in the Structure of the Brain and the Bible
Ron Levine

T HE KEY to the dilemma of our case study is in the phrase "sexual negotiation." The mindset that we bring to our sexual encounters significantly affects how satisfying they are. As one of my patients put it, "I don't want sex to be an isolated event, or even a series of isolated events. I want it to be an integral part of our relationship." Our couple's mindset as described in this case could be seen as mired in habit, beset by notions of obligation and implied judgments (different sex acts are given either the thumbs up or the thumbs down), and conceiving of these sex acts as discreet events—as if they have no relationship to the human beings that are to be engaged in them.

Though the items on Jim and Sarah's sexual "menu" are posed as potential acts of caring, this caring is framed as an intellectual agreement, not as a means of connection between loving partners. In order to effectively guide this couple to sexual satisfaction, I propose an alternate frame of reference that draws from the wisdom of both brain science and Torah in its broadest sense.

The Structure of the Brain and Sex
The brain is the largest and most potent sex organ in our bodies.[1] An understanding of how our brains function with respect to sexuality will give Jim and Sarah options they don't yet have.

The brain stem is called "the reptilian brain." Reptiles eat their young and have no sense of humor. When our reptilian brain is in charge, sexual interactions are instinctual, impulsive, and irrational. When we are in this state, anybody will do and any body will do. We have no concern about the human being with whom we are sexually involved; all we care about is gratifying our bodily urges. I call this type of sex "unfocused lust sex."

The limbic zone, another part of our brain, is also called "the mammalian brain." Mammals do not eat their young; more than that, they can bond. But this part of our brain is also characterized by intensity and instability. Our intensity in the sexual arena feels like love. In this

---

1. Gina Ogden, *The Return of Desire* (Boston, MA: Trumpeter Books, 2008), 17.

state, we focus our emotions on one individual: "I want you and only you. I love you and only you. You are the sun and the moon and the stars and all that exists ... until you don't return my text message." Then, suddenly, "love" turns to "hate." The sex that results from this state of mind is intense, exciting and unstable. Since, in this state, we focus on one individual, I call this "focused love sex," or "attraction sex." Often called "romantic love" or "infatuation," it is both exhilarating and transitory. Our emotions rapidly shift on the love-hate continuum depending on the immediate response or non-response of our partner.

Lastly, the neocortex is the part of the brain in which human thought, language, fantasy, humor, symbolic thinking, and sexual desire reside. Desire, as opposed to lust, is mental. Because of our prefrontal cortex, we are capable of symbolic thinking and imagining. We have feelings, but we also have feelings about our feelings. We have thoughts, and we also have thoughts about our thoughts. We desire, and we also desire to be desired. We want to choose our partners, and we also want to be chosen. In this state of mind, we are able to see our partner as a whole person, as opposed to just a series of behaviors. We are able to connect with his or her inner world and imagine how he or she might be feeling. We are able to commit beyond the present moment. These are the capacities that form the basis of marriage. I call the sex resulting from this state of mind "commitment sex." This type of sexual interaction and experience results from the integration of our prefrontal cortex with our limbic zone and brain stem.

If we apply this template to Jim and Sarah, we can ask the following questions: Are their requests dominated by their reptilian brain and the urge for gratification of primitive impulses, by their mammalian brain repeatedly shifting between "yes, yes," and "no, no," or by their human brain, whose integration with the lower systems allows for a more holistic approach in which sexual interaction is characterized by compassion and concern?

Put another way, when a relationship precedes sex, both the sex and the relationship are better. I look at our couple's problem as a relational problem, not as a behavioral one. The case's use of the phrases "sexual appetite" and "sexual interests" point toward the reptilian and mammalian brain systems. When we address the couple's questions from the point of view of an integrated brain, however, the issue will not be what behaviors we engage in, but rather, what these behaviors mean as an expression of a relationship.

The Garden of Eden and Sex

The Garden of Eden story in the Book of Genesis provides us with a working philosophy of sex and love. Genesis 2:7 states, "... the LORD formed [Hebrew, *yatzar*] man [Hebrew, *adam*] from the dust of the earth. He blew into his nostrils the breath [*nishmat*] of life, and man became a living being [*nefesh hayah*]." The Hebrew roots each have a dual meaning. *Yatzar* literally means "create," but its root has been interpreted in the rabbinic tradition to mean the human *desire* to create, including sexual desire. *N'shamah* means "soul," but with the addition of one letter, it also means "breath." From this, we understand that the combination of desire and soul makes us human.

In the rabbinic tradition, desire is divided into two distinct components: the good or transcendent desire and the bad, or survival- and ego-oriented desire. Both are required to create the wholeness of desire. With the integrated brain, we have the integration of differentiated states depicted as lower and higher. If we conceive of the bad and good desire as an image, it perfectly matches the tri-level sexual brain. Our self-centered desire (consisting of greed, lust, desire for instant gratification, and attraction) represents the reptilian and mammalian parts of our brain, while the transcendent desire, which allows us to connect to others in a deeper way, represents our human brain. When we add *n'shamah* (soul) into the equation, we bring the Divine element into our sexual interactions.

Our rabbinic tradition teaches that the soul is pure. Unlike desire, it has no agenda. Its only purpose is to allow for a connection from the inside out, to a life partner and to God. The word intimacy means "profoundly interior." In our intimate relationships, the writer Thomas Moore suggests, the "most within" dimensions of ourselves and the other are engaged—our deeper soul is engaged.[2]

I see this when I teach teenagers about human sexuality. I often ask them the following questions: What is your very best quality? If there is one thing you want us to know about you, what would it be? What is your greatest passion? After they share their answers, I ask: If we put

---

2. Thomas Moore, *Soul Mates* (New York: Harper Collins, 1994), 23.

these three qualities together, what would they be called? Their answer is nearly unanimous: our essence, our soul. My next question is then: In our sexual interactions, is our soul present? Or do we present a false self, an adaptive self, a seeking self?

Healthy Dialogue about Sex

I would recommend that Jim and Sarah enter into a reflective dialogue in order to come to a collaborative, relationally based, joint decision on which sexual interactions they will engage in. This reflective dialogue consists of three components: acknowledgement and affirmation; acceptance and understanding; and adding information and desire.[3]

In **acknowledgment and affirmation**, we recognize both the existence and validity of our partner's desires. We go beyond thinking about ourselves, focus on our partner, and recognize that he or she has desires that need to be satisfied as much as ours do.

In **acceptance and understanding**, we explore the nature and texture of our partner's desires. What does sexual behavior mean to them? How important is it to them? What significance does it have for them? How intensely do they feel their desires? The point of this exploration is not to have our partner justify his or her desires, but rather for us to come to a deeper understanding of our partner and experience their unique perspective. Our acceptance and understanding does not mean that we must "agree" with the desire or the desired behavior. Rather, it means that we must put it in the context of our partner's inner world.

Once this level of acknowledgment and acceptance exists, we then can **add our own opinions, thoughts, and suggestions** as we articulate our own desires. The resulting discussion is less a negotiation than it is a collaborative effort to create a joint solution. It is rare that a given desire or behavior has the same meaning or intensity for both partners. Recognizing how deeply our partner feels often allows us to engage both our compassion and our empathy.

Through reflective dialogue that incorporates all three of the factors described above, the behaviors we decide to engage in come from a place of caring for each other. It is less an intellectual act of caring and more an authentic expression of our connections with one another. This reflective

---

3. A more detailed process of sexual communication is described in "Eros and Aging" by Michael Metz and Barry McCarthy, *Psychotherapy Networker*, July–Aug. 2008, 59–60.

dialogue comes both from an integrated brain, as well as from the union of soul and desire.

As we look at the requested behaviors in this case—for example, Sarah's desire to be spanked as this is the only way she can achieve orgasm—we should remember that sex is not a goal-oriented activity, but an experiential activity. Withholding sex out of guilt, resentment or anger, or agreeing to sex out of anxiety, a compulsion to please, or a fear of not being loved, are some examples of goal-oriented sex. A couple should not use sex in pursuit of a goal, but should experience it for its own sake.

In judging the acceptability of the list of behaviors that Jim and Sarah are considering, both biblical and talmudic principles apply. The Talmud states that any sexual behavior is permitted to a married couple.[4] In Exodus 21:10, we find the concept of *onah*, according to which a husband is obligated to fulfill his wife's sexual desires. Her sexual rights in the context of marriage are clearly established. (It is interesting to note that the Talmud presumes that a man will assert his sexual rights, but a woman might not).[5] From this point of view, as long as they engage in sex in a private setting and neither is forcing the other to do anything, nothing on either person's list should be out of bounds.

For me personally, there are two notable exceptions: degrading language and engaging in a ménage à trois. If we accept that each human being is created in the image of God, degrading language is unacceptable under every circumstance, for married or unmarried couples alike. (If the couple is "acting out" degrading language as part of a mutually agreed-upon role-play or fantasy, however, that is a different story.) Additionally, if we accept that monogamy and fidelity are the cornerstones of marriage in our broader Torah tradition,[6] then a ménage à trois falls outside the bounds of monogamy. Consenting adults can do what they want, but this particular behavior is outside the bounds of marriage as it is currently Jewishly understood.

4. Daniel Boyarin, *Carnal Israel: Reading Sex in Talmudic Literature* (Berkeley, CA: University of California Press, 1995), 120.

5. David Biale, *Eros and the Jews* (Berkeley, CA: University of California Press, 1997), 154.

6. See, for example, Israel Abrahams and Joseph Jacobs, "Monogamy," in *The Jewish Encyclopedia* (New York: Funk and Wagnalls, 1906). Available at http://www. jewishencyclopedia.com/view.jsp?artid=730&letter=M&search=monogamy.

If we accept the principles of an integrated brain, together with the values of Torah as guides for our sexual interactions, then our sexual decision making should reflect them both. We can consider the purpose of sexual interaction before engaging in it, fully experience it while we engage in it, and savor the experience afterward. This creates a full, complete, and satisfying sexual interaction regardless of the particular behaviors that we choose to engage in.

A Bit of Heaven Here on Earth
Mark Dratch

F EW THINGS in our lives are more complicated than sex. It is both a simple physical act and a complex emotional, personal, social, and religious experience. It is a dynamic mix of physical pleasure, libidinous desire, emotional pulls, psychological baggage, and personal agendas: With whom will I have sex? When will I have sex for the first time? When will I have sex with a new partner or with a spouse? Where will we do it? What kinds of sexual activities will we engage in? What is my motivation for having sex: pleasure, pressure, lust, desire, obligation, routine? Do I want to have sex? How do I satisfy myself? How do I satisfy my partner?

Sex is also complicated because it is not just about "me"; it is a shared activity. Engaging in sexual intercourse with concern only about one's own satisfaction is tantamount to masturbating in front of someone; it is selfish and demeaning to the other person. We need to be aware of and concerned about the desires and needs of another, often keeping our own needs and sexual expression in check. In addition, baring ourselves in front of another person—literally and figuratively—makes us vulnerable and exposes us physically, emotionally, and psychologically. And sex is complicated because while sexual relations can contribute to the intimate nature of a relationship, creating bonds of mutual trust, understanding, and love, they can also communicate a whole set of messages, different for different genders and for different individuals, that we may or may not mean to communicate.

Applying Jewish Law and Values to Sex
For those of us who embrace Judaism as a way of life, with a unique worldview and as a framework that guides all aspects of who we are and what we do (through the observance of *halakhah*, Jewish law), sex has a uniquely Jewish context. Values and insights of a tradition that are simultaneously divine and human, spiritual and psychological, direct our behavior. Judaism has very significant things to contribute to our lives, including to our relationships with others, which can elevate us morally and sanctify us spiritually. In addition, the objectivity of Jewish law can protect us from the subjective pushes and pulls of our active libidos, which often cloud good judgment.

The Torah does not shy away from any subject. God created both our souls and our bodies, and has much to say about sexual matters including

133

marriage and divorce, incest, homosexuality, *niddah* (sexual relations during menses), *mikveh* (the Jewish ritual bath),[1] adultery, rape,[2] and more. For Jews, sex is not inherently evil, nor is it merely tolerated only for the sake of procreation. For us, sex is about intimacy, mutual respect, modesty, pleasure, and even holiness and spirituality. And Judaism is aware of the value of the libido in all aspects of our lives.

In fact, married couples are not just permitted to be intimate with each other, a husband is obligated to have sex with his wife—the mitzvah is called *onah*.[3] And while no biblical verse commands a wife to sleep with her husband, many suggest that it is intuitively part and parcel of the institution of marriage.[4]

There are two trends in classical Jewish thinking about sexual behavior. One of them is prudent and restrictive, limiting the frequency with which husbands and wives may be intimate and restricting the nature of sexual activities in which they may engage.[5] The other trend is more liberal and permissive, allowing a wide range of sexual expression, so long as both parties consent.[6] The more permissive opinion also emphasizes modesty, respect, and restraint.[7] Rabbi Yohanan of the Talmud observed: "Man has a small organ: starve it, it is satisfied; satisfy it, it is starved."[8] The rabbis feared that too much focus on sexual activity could create an unhealthy preoccupation with the carnal and physical elements of life.

The defining principles that govern all interpersonal interactions, especially sexual ones, include *tzeniu't* (modesty), *kedushah* (holiness), *derekh eretz* (decency), *kevod ha-beriyot* (dignity), *tzelem Elohim* (the image of God in which all humans are created), *hesed* (kindness), and *ahavat re'im* (neighborly love). These values are especially important in matters of love and sex. True love enhances the other's self-esteem, dignity and feeling of self-worth, and sex is a significant expression of that love. In fact, these values complete the physical pleasures and satisfaction

1. See Maimonides (Rambam), *Mishneh Torah*, Hilkhot Mikva'ot 1:2, for example.
2. Rape is most fundamentally a crime of violence. However, it is expressed through sexual acts, and as such has elements and consequences related to issues of sexuality.
3. Based on Exodus 21:10; Maimonides, Hilkhot Ishut 14:7.
4. Shlomo ben Aderet (Rashba) to *Nedarim* 15b.
5. See *Shulchan Arukh*, *Orach Chayyim* 240.
6. Babylonian Talmud, *Nedarim* 20b.
7. *Shulchan Arukh*, *Even ha-Ezer* 25:2.
8. Babylonian Talmud, *Sukkah* 52b.

enjoyed through sexual intimacy, not only elevating them, but making them enduring. Our rabbis explained that the dignity of *kevod ha-beriyot* is due to everyone because of the *tzelem Elohim* (image of God) in which each of us was created.[9] By grounding human dignity in Divine dignity, any slight or act of disrespect to a human being becomes an affront to God. By respecting others, our relationship with them becomes holy.

The Meaning of Consent

Jim and Sarah face an important challenge. They are happily married but have different sexual preferences and, as a result, each is less than sexually satisfied. Their marriage is strained: her interests and requests make her husband uncomfortable, and his demands discomfort her too. Their marriage may be vulnerable, and the welfare of their children could be at stake. How much should Sarah sacrifice? How far should Jim compromise?

In a reversal of the stereotype that it is women who are usually pressured to engage in sexual activities more often or in ways that make them uneasy, in this case it is Jim who feels pressure to engage in behaviors with which he is personally uncomfortable. Simply put—although here, as in many areas of life, nothing is really so simple—Jewish law rules that people should engage in sexual relations willingly; it prohibits a husband to force his wife to have intercourse.[10] And the bar for consent is set high. Even if a wife is not forced to participate in sexual activity, as long as she is not fully agreeable to intercourse, sexual relations are prohibited.[11] All of this means that if a husband or wife is interested in having sex, it is his or her responsibility to seduce the partner and

---

9. See Genesis 1:26. For more on the connection between *tzelem Elohim* and *kavod ha-beriyot*, see Mark Dratch, "The Divine Honor Roll: Kevod ha-Beriyot (Human Dignity) in Jewish Law and Thought." Available at http://jsafe.org/pdfs/Kevod_Habriyot.pdf.

10. Babylonian Talmud, *Eruvin* 100b: "Rami b. Hama citing R. Assi further ruled: 'A man is forbidden to compel his wife to the [marital] obligation, since it is said in Scripture: "Without consent the soul is not good; and he that hurries with his feet sins" (Proverbs 19:2).'" Ba'ailei ha-Nefesh, Sha'ar ha-Kedushah; Maimonides, *Mishneh Torah,* Hilkhot De'ot 5:4, Hilkhot Ishut 15:17; *Shulchan Arukh, Even ha-Ezer* 25:2. See Warren Goldstein, *Defending the Human Spirit: Jewish Law's Vision for a Moral Society* (New York: Feldheim, 2006), 151–220.

11. *Magen Avraham, Orach Chayyim* 240, no. 7; Zohar, Bereshit 49b, 148b, Va-yikra 225b. Maimonides, Hilkhot Ishut 15:17, rules, "[Her husband] should not coerce her [to have relations] when she does not desire to do so. Rather, [they should engage in intercourse only] when there is mutual desire and pleasure." Masekhet Kallah Rabbati 1:11; *Shulchan Arukh, Orach Chayyim* 240 and *Even ha-Ezer* 25.

earn consent.[12] However, if these advances are rebuffed, they must be stopped. No means no.

Nonconsensual sex is rape, and Jewish law recognizes the concept of marital rape; a man may not force his wife to have intercourse.[13] The Talmud even labels some marital intercourse as *anusah* (rape) and *eimah* (coerced out of fear).[14] An important medieval rabbinic authority rules that a wife should not be forced to have sex because "she is not a captive to be sexually ravished at her husband's whim."[15] This position of Jewish law—forbidding marital rape—is almost as revolutionary today as it was thousands of years ago. Today, marital rape accounts for approximately 25% of all rapes and is experienced by 10–14% of married women. Shamefully, it was not until July 1993 that marital rape became a crime in all 50 states. In 17 states and the District of Columbia, there are no exemptions from rape prosecution granted to husbands, but in 33 states some exemptions still exist.[16]

While the case of Jim and Sarah is not one of marital rape, it does deal with issues of consent. Is a full and unconditional "yes" always required?

---

12. In *Iggeret ha-Kodesh*, chapter 6, ascribed to Nahmanides (Ramban), we find the following guidance: "When a man has relations [with his wife] he should not do so against her will and he should not rape her; the Divine Presence does not abide in such unions in as much as his intentions are in opposition to hers, and she does not consent to his desire. He should not quarrel with her or strike her in order to force marital relations. Behold, the Sages said (Pesahim 49b), 'Just as a lion tears [his prey] and devours it and has no shame, so an *'am ha-'arez* (ignorant boor) strikes and cohabits and has no shame.' Instead, he should entice her with kind and alluring words and other proper and reputable things. He should not have relations with her while she is sleeping because their intentions are not united and they are not of the same mind. Rather, he should wake her and arouse her with conversation. The bottom line is this: when a man is sexually aroused he should make sure that his wife is aroused as well [before having intercourse]."

13. Babylonian Talmud, *Eruvin* 100b: "Rami b. Hama citing R. Assi further ruled: 'A man is forbidden to compel his wife to the [marital] obligation, since it is said in Scripture: "Without consent the soul is not good; and he that hurries with his feet sins" (Proverbs 19:2)'"; *Ba'alei ha-Nefesh, Sha'ar ha-Kedushah*; Maimonides, *Mishneh Torah*, Hilkhot De'ot 5:4; *Even ha-Ezer* 25:2. See Mark Dratch, "I Do? Consent and Coercion in Sexual Relations" in *Rav Chesed: Essays in Honor of Rabbi Dr. Haskel Lookstein*, R. Medoff, ed. (Jersey City, NJ: Ktav, 2009), 119–144.

14. Babylonian Talmud, *Nedarim* 20b.

15. Teshuvot Maharit I, 5.

16. When his wife is legally unable to consent due to mental or physical impairment or if she is unconscious or asleep, a husband is exempt from prosecution in many of these 33 states. See http://www.vawnet.org/DomesticViolence/ Research/VAWnetDocs/AR_mrape.pdf.

Such a standard is impossible to support, as achieving complete mutual consent at all times is unrealistic. Husbands and wives have different desires. They have different needs at different times, and have different expectations of themselves and of their partners. At times, a spouse says "yes" even if he or she does not really want to.

Rev. Marie Fortune, Founder and Senior Analyst at the FaithTrust Institute, an international multi-faith organization that addresses issues of abuse in religious communities, observes that, "... acquiescence may pose as 'consent,' but it is not the same."[17] In other words, a person may engage in "altruistic" sex—sex just to keep a partner satisfied. When agreeing to sex for altruistic motives, we are not coerced, we just have a desire to maintain *shalom bayit* (an agreeable relationship) or to avoid a fight. This situation is certainly not ideal, but it is real, and as long as it does not reflect the totality of a couple's sexual relationship, such accommodation may be necessary for the relationship's long-term health.

So, on a given evening, if one partner wants to have sex and the other does not, does the disinterested partner have an obligation to acquiesce to the sexual needs of the other? I would say yes, as long as this is not a defining issue in their relationship and as long as that partner does not have serious objections to having sex that particular evening. People marry for many reasons; having sex is one of them. They have, according to Jewish law, a commitment to have sex and a reasonable expectation that they and their partner will engage in sexual activity.

When Violations of Dignity Nullify Consent

The concerns are different when we consider the other sexual behaviors over which Jim and Sarah disagree. First, even the more liberal school of thought in Jewish tradition, which allows for a wide range of sexual expression, requires mutual consent. And, second, we are dealing here with fetishes such as demeaning talk, spanking, and sado-masochism, which are by their very nature and design degrading. These kinds of behaviors violate the principles outlined above of dignity, respect, and modesty. They are, in fact, a violation of *kevod ha-beriyot*, the universal standards of dignity and respect that are due to everyone. Because respect for *kevod ha-beriyot* is really respect for God, as humans are

---

17. Marie Fortune, *Sexual Violence: The Sin Revisited* (Cleveland, OH: The Pilgrim Press, 2005), 56.

created in the divine image, this is not a subjective matter. Just because I want something and I do not consider it degrading to me does not mean that it is not a violation of human dignity.

Such behaviors may be violations of the letter and spirit of Jewish law, as well. The verse, "Do not wrong one another" (Lev. 25:17) prohibits me from causing any kind of emotional distress to another person. This is called *ona'at devarim* (verbal wronging), under which rabbinic interpretation includes not only speech, but any action that damages others' emotional well-being[18] or causes them emotional or psychological pain.[19] The rabbis of the Talmud punished the sage R. Rehumi for causing his wife to cry because they knew how damaging the emotional pain one person inflicts on another can be.[20] Furthermore, physical violence is prohibited by the Torah. Not only may we not harm another, we may not harm ourselves.[21] Even raising a hand against anyone in a threatening way is outlawed.[22]

Technically, these acts—*ona'at devarim* and assault—are prohibited only if they are committed in a malicious or harmful manner. If they are done to achieve a positive benefit, they may be permissible. In this case, Sarah and Jim claim that these acts will give them sexual pleasure. However, these acts are not benign; they violate the spirit of the law, which frowns on violence, aggression, and cruelty. They are

---

18. See Rashi to Leviticus 25:17.
19. See Rashi, *Bava Metzi'a* 59b, s.v. *hutz*; Maimonides, Sefer ha-Mitzvot, no. 251.
20. Babylonian Talmud, *Ketubbot* 62b.
21. Maimonides, *Mishneh Torah*, Hilkhot Shevu'ot 5:17, Hilkhot Hovel u-Mazik 5:1; *Bava Kamma* 92a: "If one says, 'Put out my eye, cut off my arm or break my leg,' the offender would nevertheless be liable; [and so also even if he told him to do it] on the understanding that he would be exempt, he would still be liable."
22. Babylonian Talmud, *Sanhedrin* 58b, derives this from the encounter between Moses and the Hebrew slaves he confronted while first exploring Egypt: "And he said unto the wicked man, 'Why would you hit your friend?'" (Exodus 2:13). The Talmud explains: "'Why have you hit' is not said, but 'why will you hit,' showing that though he had not hit him yet, [the would-be perpetrator] is called wicked. Ze'iri said in R. Hanina's name: 'He is called a sinner, for it is written, "But if not, I will take it by force" (1 Samuel 2:16), and it is further written, "Wherefore the sin of the young men was very great before the Lord" (2:16).' R. Huna said: 'His hand should be cut off, as it is written, "Let the uplifted arm be broken" (Job 38:15).' R. Huna had the hand cut off [of one who was accustomed to strike other people]. R. Elazar said: 'The only thing to be done with him is to bury him, as it is written, "And a man of [uplifted] arm, for him is the earth" (Job 22:8).'" Maimonides, *Mishneh Torah*, Hilkhot Hovel u-Mazik 5:2; *Shulchan Arukh, Hoshen Mishpat* 420:1.

also harmful to this relationship. While Sarah likes to be spanked, Jim personally finds the thought of spanking his wife to be degrading to her. What may appear to be a positive benefit to one partner causes hurtful distress to the other.

Degrading speech, slapping, sado-masachism and the like are degrading acts and are a violation of the human dignity of both the actor and the person being acted upon. We may not violate others' dignity, and we may not violate our own either. It is for this reason, suggests Rabbi Joseph Soloveitchik, that Jewish law compares those who behave in undignified ways to dogs.[23] We must insist that others treat us with respect. The first Chief Rabbi of pre-State Israel, Rabbi Abraham Isaac Kook, insisted that "protecting [the respect] one rightfully deserves is not a matter of arrogance; on the contrary, there is a mitzvah to do so."[24]

Finally, cross-dressing and ménage à trois are both violations of biblical prohibitions. Deuteronomy 22:5 prohibits cross-dressing, especially when done to elicit erotic pleasure.[25] And marriage is designed to be monogamous and modest: the Ten Commandments ban adultery,[26] even when consensual. A person may not think of one person while being intimate with another;[27] and a couple may not have intercourse, a private and intimate act that demands modesty, when someone else is present.[28] Jewish law prohibits someone from even sleeping in the same room with a married couple for fear that another's presence might restrain the couple from intimacy.[29] These forbidden acts are viewed as violations of the mandates of respect, dignity, and modesty owed to one's partner and due to oneself.

A Bit of Heaven on Earth

The case of Jim and Sarah challenges us to understand the complexities of sexual relations; of our own personal needs and those of our partner; of the impact of sex on a relationship; of the long-term commitment, investment, and sacrifice needed to help a marriage succeed; of the impact of

---

23. Babylonian Talmud, *Kiddushin* 40b. See Rabbi Joseph Soloveitchik, *The Lonely Man of Faith* (New York: Doubleday, 1992), 13; and *Yemei Zikaron*, p. 20.
24. *Mussar Avikha* (Jerusalem, 5731), 73.
25. See Rashi to Deuteronomy 22:5.
26. Exodus 20:13.
27. *Shulchan Arukh*, *Orach Chayyim* 240:2.
28. *Shulchan Arukh*, *Orach Chayyim* 240:6.
29. Babylonian Talmud, *Eruvin* 63b; *Shulchan Arukh*, *Even ha-Ezer* 25:5; Mishneh Brurah to *Orach Chayyim* 240:52.

our behavior on our own emotional and spiritual well-being and on the well-being of another; of our own personal dignity; and of our moral and religious development. The issues are not simple and their resolutions are not easy, but Jewish ideals and ethics offer a framework in which we can evaluate our values and behaviors. In doing so, we may yet elevate our interests beyond the demands of our fleeting urges and desires. And we may yet find a way, even through enjoying the pleasures of the physical world, to taste the bliss of the infinite world of eternity, a bit of Heaven right here on earth.

Conclusion: The Ethics of Sex

THERE IS a story in the Babylonian Talmud (Berakhot 62a) about a curious student who takes his studies past the point of what might generally be considered good taste. Kahane, the yeshiva boy in question, hides under the bed of his teacher, deliberately listening in on the master's lovemaking with his wife. He is shocked by the way they chat and joke together during the coital act, but tries his best to remain unnoticed. To no avail, however, as in one dramatic moment, his presence—and chutzpah—are revealed.

"Kahane, are you there?" his teacher thunders. "Leave now, because it is rude!"

Kahane calmly replies that it is not rude at all and that he will not leave, "For this is Torah, and I must learn."

In Judaism, every aspect of human life is a holy piece of Torah, worthy of thought, study, and consideration—and sex is certainly no exception. And yet, as the essays in this volume have amply demonstrated, it is no small task to figure out what that view means on the ground, how to translate our aspirations for a sacred sexuality to the messy, complex reality of our interpersonal lives. How to do this sensibly and ethically was not even clear to Kahane's teacher, Rav, one of the great rabbinic minds of Jewish history. How much more difficult must it be for us!

In our lives today, some of the questions are age-old—perhaps the same ones with which Kahane and his peers struggled—and some are more challenging than they have ever been. A decade or two of dating, extended programs of education, high divorce rates, and a whole host of new STDs have generally replaced the model of arranged marriages and marrying young, the pattern that was prevalent in Jewish culture for over 2,000 years. But the human heart and body remain, as ever, the same. As such, the issues raised in this book involve both traditional and highly contemporary ways of thinking.

What are our obligations to those we are casually dating? How can two people with distinct differences in desire and arousal come together in a mutually satisfying way? Might how we handle issues around the unforeseen consequences of sex depend on whether the relationship is short-term or committed? Do the current complexities of capitalism and economic opportunity impact the way we understand sex work? The answers are far from clear-cut; hence the diversity of voices found in these pages.

Furthermore, underlying these questions is a whole host of other questions: What is the relationship between sex and love? Are they completely independent? Are they interdependent? If there is a connection between these things, what should it look like? Certainly, it is possible to have sex without love and love without sex, but as the Babylonian Talmud (Nedarim 20b) notes, sexuality devoid of any connection whatsoever to the person with whom we are sexual has the potential to leave us feeling used up and empty. It quotes one rabbi who asserts metaphorically that "one must not drink from one cup and think of another," and condemns sexual relations that take place when either partner is angry, is drunk, is confused about the identity of the other partner, hates the other partner, has decided to leave the relationship, is in the middle of an argument with the other partner, or is in any one of a number of other situations that might prevent both people from being entirely present with each other, fully in the moment of connection, and engaged not only physically, but emotionally as well. The 13th-century rabbi and philosopher Nahmanides told a prospective groom to "bring together your thought with her thought and your intention with hers" (Iggeret ha-Kodesh, ch. 6).

The 20th-century theologian Martin Buber wrote of two different kinds of relationships, two ways of interacting with others. He defined "I-It" relationships as those in which the other is regarded as little more than an object at one's disposal—a server is considered the object that brings food, a cab driver the object that drives to the airport. An "I-Thou" relationship, on the other hand, is one in which the other person is regarded as a whole being, full of hopes and dreams and selfhood, as created in the Divine Image, and in which the relationship is not bounded by a utilitarian framework. I-Thou relationships have no pre-set boundaries and are modeled upon our relationship with the Divine. In all situations, this is the ideal for our interactions with other people. This is especially what we should strive to achieve in building long-term, intimate relationships.

One thing that clearly emerges from the Jewish tradition is that it prizes intentionality, responsibility, and integrity in all areas of one's life, including one's sex life. What this means for each individual in the choices that he or she makes will vary, but the lens through which one considers his or her sexual choices should include these values—of regarding the other as a "Thou," not as an instrument to achieve some goal, sexual or otherwise; of being morally responsible in our sexual acts as in all other areas of life; and of being fully present in our sexual relationships.

This book has introduced a series of ancient and modern Jewish voices on sexuality and sexual activity. They are as diverse and complex as one might hope from a tradition that highly values discussion, debate, and multiple points of view. Here, as in many areas of life, there are no easy answers, and there are important considerations on all sides. And even though it is, at times, rather hard work, it is incumbent upon us to sort through the many ways of approaching questions about sex and intimacy. Only then can we devise a Jewish sexual ethic that reflects our highest aspirations for ourselves, for those with whom we share our most intimate moments, and, perhaps, for God as well.

For this, too, is Torah.

Suggestions for Further Reading

On Sex and Love

Aviv, Caryn and Schneer, David, eds. *Queer Jews.* New York: Routledge, 2002.

Biale, David. *Eros and the Jews: From Biblical Israel to Contemporary America.* Berkeley, CA: University of California Press, 1997.

Borowitz, Eugene. *Choosing A Sex Ethic: A Jewish Inquiry.* New York: Schocken Books, 1969.

Boteach, Shmuel (Shmuley). *Kosher Sex: A Recipe for Passion and Intimacy.* London: Duckworth Press, 1998.

———. *Dating Secrets of the Ten Commandments.* New York: Doubleday, 2000.

Dorff, Elliot. *Love Your Neighbor and Yourself.* Philadelphia: The Jewish Publication Society, 2003, especially chapter 3.

Friedman, Avraham Peretz. *Marital Intimacy: A Traditional Jewish Approach.* Northvale, NJ: Jason Aronson, 1996.

Furman, Leah. *Single Jewish Female: A Modern Guide to Sex and Dating.* New York: Perigree, 2004.

Gold, Michael. *Does God Belong in the Bedroom?* Philadelphia: The Jewish Publication Society, 1992.

Gordis, Robert. *Love and Sex: A Modern Jewish Perspective, 2nd edition.* New York: Hippocrene Books, 1988.

Greenberg, Steven. *Wrestling With God and Men: Homosexuality in the Jewish Tradition.* Madison, WI: University of Wisconsin Press, 2005.

Lamm, Maurice. *The Jewish Way in Love and Marriage.* San Francisco: Harper and Row, 1980.

Magnonet, Jonathan, ed. *Jewish Explorations of Sexuality.* Providence, RI: Berghahn Books, 1995.

Michaelson, Jay. *God in Your Body: Kabbalah, Mindfulness, and Embodied Spiritual Practice.* Woodstock, VT: Jewish Lights, 2007, especially chapter 6.

Plaskow, Judith. *The Coming of Lilith: Essays on Feminism, Judaism and Sexual Ethics, 1972–2003.* Boston: Beacon Press, 2005.

Roffman, Deborah M. *Sex and Sensibility: The Thinking Parent's Guide to Talking Sense About Sex.* Cambridge, MA: Da Capo Press, 2001.

Ruttenberg, Danya. *The Passionate Torah: Sex and Judaism*. New York: New York University Press, 2009.

Waskow, Arthur. *Down-to-Earth Judaism: Food, Money, Sex and the Rest of Life*. New York: William Morrow and Co., 1995.

Westheimer, Ruth K. and Jonathan Mark. *Heavenly Sex: Sexuality in the Jewish Tradition*. New York: New York University Press, 1995.

Winkler, Gershon. *Sacred Secrets: The Sanctity of Sex in Jewish Law and Lore*. Northvale, NJ: Jason Aronson (now Lanham, MD: Rowman and Littlefield), 1998.

Yedwab, Paul. *Sex in the Texts*. New York: UAHC Press, 2001.

On Contraception and Abortion

Dorff, Elliot N. *Matters of Life and Death: A Jewish Approach to Modern Medical Ethics*. Philadelphia: The Jewish Publication Society, 1998, especially chapters 3–6. (The officially adopted Conservative approach to infertility, contraception, and abortion.)

Feldman, David M. *Marital Relations, Birth Control, and Abortion in Jewish Law*. New York: Schocken Books, 1974 (originally 1968, New York University Press).

Feldman, Emanuel and Joel B. Wolowelsky, eds. *Jewish Law and the New Reproductive Technologies*. Hoboken, NJ: KTAV, 1997. (An Orthodox approach to infertility.)

Millen, Rochelle L. *Women, Birth, and Death in Jewish Law and Practice*. Hanover, NH: University of New England Press, 2004, especially chapter 2.

Schiff, Daniel. *Abortion in Judaism*. New York: Cambridge University Press, 2002.

Washofsky, Mark. *Jewish Living: A Guide to Contemporary Reform Practice*. New York: UAHC Press, 2001, especially pp. 233–245. (The officially adopted Reform approach to infertility, contraception, and abortion.)

Editors and Contributors

Editors

Elliot N. Dorff, rabbi (The Jewish Theological Seminary), Ph.D. (Columbia University), is rector and Sol and Anne Dorff Distinguished Professor of Philosophy at the American Jewish University in Los Angeles. Among the 12 books he has written are three award-winning books on Jewish ethics published by The Jewish Publication Society: *Matters of Life and Death* (1998), *To Do the Right and the Good* (2002), and *Love Your Neighbor and Yourself* (2003). He has also edited 10 books, including *Contemporary Jewish Ethics and Morality* (Oxford, 1995) and *Contemporary Jewish Theology* (Oxford, 1999). *Contemporary Jewish Theology* was co-edited by Louis Newman, who also co-edited the first three volumes of the *Jewish Choices, Jewish Voices* series. Since 1984, Dorff has served on the Rabbinical Assembly's Committee on Jewish Law and Standards, and has served as its Chair since 2007. He has also served on several federal advisory commissions dealing with the ethics of health care, sexual responsibility, and research on human subjects and is a member of the State of California's Ethics Committee on embryonic stem cell research. He and his wife, Marlynn, have four children and seven grandchildren.

Danya Ruttenberg, rabbi (Ziegler School of Rabbinic Studies, American Jewish University), is the author of *Surprised By God: How I Learned to Stop Worrying and Love Religion* (Beacon Press, 2008), and editor of *The Passionate Torah: Sex and Judaism* (NYU Press, 2009) and *Yentl's Revenge: The Next Wave of Jewish Feminism* (Seal Press, 2001). She is also a contributing editor to *Lilith* and to the academic journal *Women and Judaism*, is on the editorial board of (and blogs at) Jewschool.com, and has been published in many books and periodicals over the years. Ruttenberg, who lives in the Boston area with her husband and son, serves as the Senior Jewish Educator at Tufts University and teaches and lectures nationwide.

Contributors

Martha Ackelsberg, Ph.D. (Princeton University), is a long-time Jewish feminist activist and a founding member of both Ezrat Nashim and B'not Esh. As the William R. Kenan, Jr., Professor of Government and of the Study of Women and Gender at Smith College, her teaching focuses on women's activism, feminist and democratic theory, and community politics. In addition to numerous articles and book chapters, she is author of *Free Women of Spain: Anarchism and the Struggle for the Emancipation of Women*

(AK Press, 2005) and of *Resisting Citizenship: Feminist Essays on Politics, Community and Democracy* (Routledge, 2009). She also lectures and leads workshops on topics that include Jewish women's activism, feminist transformations of Jewish life, and reconceptualizing families.

S. Bear Bergman is an author and a theater artist. He is the author of *Butch Is a Noun* (Suspect Thoughts Press, 2006) and *The Nearest Exit May Be Behind You* (Arsenal Pulp, 2009), and of three award-winning solo performances. He is also a frequent contributor to anthologies on all manner of topics, from the sacred to the extremely profane. A longtime educator, Bergman continues to work at the points of intersection between gender, sexuality, and culture. His website is: www.sbearbergman.com.

Hanne Blank is a writer and historian whose work centers on issues of gender and sexuality. The author of numerous books, including *Virgin: The Untouched History* (Bloomsbury, 2008) and *Straight*, a history of heterosexuality, to be published by Beacon Press.

Gabriel Blau, an activist and writer, is the founder of The God & Sexuality Conference, an annual academic conference on religion, sexuality and gender. He has spoken and taught in the U.S. and Israel at various institutions, including Columbia, New York, Yale, and Wesleyan Universities, The Rothko Chapel, Machon Schechter, and Eylat Chayim. He is on the board of Congregation Beth Simchat Torah, New York's synagogue for LGBTQ Jews, a member of the Advisory Committee of the LGBT Religious Archives Network at the Center for Lesbian and Gay Studies and Ministry at Pacific College of Religion, and a member of the faculty of Nehirim: GLBT Jewish Culture and Spirituality. Blau received his Bachelor's in Theology from Bard College and studied at the Conservative Yeshiva in Jerusalem. He is a partner at Visible Shops, an Internet marketing firm, and lives in Manhattan with his husband and son.

Jeffrey Burack, M.D. (Harvard Medical School), is Medical Director of the East Bay AIDS Center in Oakland, CA, which provides comprehensive medical care to a diverse population of 1,500 patients with HIV/AIDS. He is an Associate Clinical Professor of Bioethics and Medical Humanities at the UC-Berkeley School of Public Health and an Associate Clinical Professor of Medicine at UC-San Francisco. He also chairs the Ethics Committee at Alta Bates Summit Medical Center in Berkeley. After graduating from Harvard University in 1981 with a degree in Biology, he studied moral philosophy as a Rhodes Scholar at the University of Oxford, from which he received the graduate B.Phil. degree. He returned to Harvard, where concurrently with his medical studies, he received a Master of Public Policy from the John F. Kennedy School of Government as the Knowles Scholar in Health Policy. Burack lives in Berkeley, CA with his wife and three children.

Aimee Dinschel, M.S.W. (The University of Illinois at Chicago), has spent the last several years doing both direct service and policy-level advocacy work with women who have been negatively impacted by the sex trade.

Mark Dratch, rabbi (Rabbi Isaac Elchanan Theological Seminary, Yeshiva University), is the founder and CEO of JSafe: The Jewish Institute Supporting an Abuse-Free Environment, and an instructor in Jewish Studies and Philosophy at Yeshiva University in New York City. Dratch serves on the leadership team of FaithTrust Institute and on the Clergy Advisory Board of Jewish Women International. He also served as a pulpit rabbi for 22 years.

Rachel Durchslag is a trustee of the Nathan Cummings Foundation and is the founder and director of the Chicago Alliance Against Sexual Exploitation, an organization that works to eliminate the demand for individuals in the sex trade through prevention, public awareness and intervention.

Steven Edelman-Blank, rabbi (Ziegler School of Rabbinic Studies, American Jewish University), is the Rabbi of Tifereth Israel Synagogue in Des Moines, Iowa. A graduate of Harvard University, he also edited the Contemporary Sources of the first three volumes of the *Jewish Choices/Jewish Voices* series.

Gloria Feldt is a leading advocate for women's health and women's rights. She is the author of two books on reproductive health and justice: *Behind Every Choice Is a Story* (University of North Texas Press, 2003) and *The War on Choice* (Bantam, 2004). She is also the co-author (with Kathleen Turner) of *Send Yourself Roses: Thoughts on Life, Love, and Leading Roles* (Springboard, 2008). The granddaughter of Eastern European Jewish immigrants who settled in small Texas towns, she has been called "the voice of experience" by *People Magazine.* She rose to serve as president of Planned Parenthood Federation of America, the nation's largest provider of reproductive health care. Prior to that, she was CEO of Planned Parenthood of West Texas and of Planned Parenthood of Central and Northern Arizona. She has written numerous articles and op-eds that have appeared in major national media such as *The New York Times, Salon.com,* and *Elle Magazine,* and penned chapters for five books, including *Our Bodies, Ourselves: Menopause* (Touchstone, 2006). She has appeared on many major news shows, from *Today* and *Hardball* to *The Daily Show with Jon Stewart,* and serves on the boards of the Women's Media Center and the Jewish Women's Archive.

Ron Jeremy was born Ron Jeremy Hyatt in 1953, in Queens, NY. He received a master's degree from Queens College and began teaching special education classes in the New York City area. In 1978, a girlfriend sent his photo off to *Playgirl* magazine for an appearance in its "Boy Next Door" pages, and since then, Jeremy has gone on to become the number one U.S. male star of adult cinema. He is still appearing in front of the camera in adult films and has attained iconic status in the adult entertainment industry.

Esther D. Kustanowitz writes, edits and consults on matters relating to Jewish life, pop culture, dating and relationships, and online social media. She wrote "First Person Singular," a singles column in New York's *The Jewish Week* for more than four years. She currently blogs at My Urban Kvetch and at Jdaters Anonymous. Kustanowitz also consults for the ROI Community, an international network of young Jewish innovators in their 20s and 30s, and has been known to teach improv. She lives in Los Angeles, CA.

Ron Levine, rabbi (The Jewish Theological Seminary of America), Ph.D. (California School of Professional Psychology), is a practicing clinical psychologist in Van Nuys, California. Formerly a teacher at the Los Angeles Hebrew High School, an instructor in education at the University of Judaism, and the director of Camp Ramah in California, his particular areas of interest include marital relationships, sexuality, and parent-child relationships. He is a member of the Society for the Scientific Study of Sexuality and the American Association of Counselors, Sex Educators and Therapists. He is currently writing and teaching a curriculum for juniors and seniors at the Los Angeles Hebrew High School entitled: "Torah and Brain Science: An Integrated Approach to Human Sexuality." He also teaches brain science and sex to 6th, 7th, 8th, and 10th grade students at two private schools in the Van Nuys area.

Scott Perlo, rabbi (Ziegler School of Rabbinic Studies, American Jewish University), is the Rabbi in Residence of the Professional Leaders Project. His adventures as a student took him across the country and around the world, most notably to Poland, where he spent an extraordinary summer as the student rabbi of Beit Warszawa, a small congregation in Warsaw. He has traveled to El Salvador with the American Jewish World Service and to Bethlehem and Hebron with Encounter, and has worked for Hillel at UCLA, Los Angeles Hebrew High School, and Camp Ramah. He was a fellow at the Kollel of the Conservative Yeshiva in Jerusalem and was the rabbinic intern of IKAR, a Jewish spiritual community in West Los Angeles.

Deborah M. Roffman, M.S. (Towson University), is a nationally certified human sexuality and family life educator who teaches sexuality education to students in grades 4–12 in Baltimore. She is the author of *Sex and Sensibility: The Thinking Parents Guide to Talking Sense about Sex* (Perseus, 2001) and has worked as a presenter and consultant for schools and parent groups across the country for more than three decades. She and her husband are active members of the Chizuk Amuno Congregation.

Uzi Weingarten, rabbi (Rabbi Isaac Elchanan Theological Seminary, Yeshiva University), leads seminars in effective, heart-centered communication. He earned a master's degree in Jewish Education from Yeshiva University, and teaches Torah with an emphasis on the message of the Prophets and modern-day psychological insights, focusing on what we can learn to improve our human interactions and spiritual awareness. His website is www.cwcseminars.com.

Index

Index

STDs
    and prostitutes, 85
    disclosing, 18, 42, 51, 61–62, 66–70
    ignorance of infection, 66
    Jewish ethical sources on, 40–43
    prevention of, 41–42, 64, 71
    stigma of, 61, 66–67
    testing for, 51, 65–67
stereotypes, 54, 60, 93, 94
strip clubs
    drug use in, 99–100
    patrons of, 79, 100–102, 109–110
    prostitution in, 99–100, 107
    working conditions in, 98–101, 107
submission. *see* BDSM

W

wages, paying, 77–78, 94
women
    appearance of in work place, 91
    Jewish, and pornography, 90
    limiting sexual behavior, 92–93
    remuneration from sex work, 83–84, 98–99
    sexual autonomy of, 8, 80, 93–94, 105
    use of contraception, 50

Z

zonah, 4